Couples
Group
Psychotherapy

A CLINICAL PRACTICE MODEL

Couples
Group
Psychotherapy

A CLINICAL PRACTICE MODEL

Judith Coché, Ph.D.

AND

Erich Coché, Ph.D.

BRUNNER/MAZEL, *A member of the Taylor & Francis Group*

Library of Congress Cataloging-in-Publication Data
Coché, Judith.
    Couples group psychotherapy : a clinical practice model / by
Judith Coché and Erich Coché.
        p.   cm.
    Includes bibliographical references.
    Includes index.
    ISBN 0-87630-598-2
    1. Marital psychotherapy.   2. Group psychotherapy.   I. Coché,
Erich.   II. Title.
    [DNLM: 1. Marital Therapy—methods.   2. Psychotherapy, Group-
methods.   WM 55 C661c]
RC488.5.C62   1990
616.89′156—dc20
DNLM/DLC
for Library of Congress   90-2216
                                                                            CIP

Brunner/Mazel
A member of the Taylor & Francis Group
47 Runway Road, Suite G
Levittown, PA 19057-4700

Manufactured in the United States of America

10 9 8 7 6 5 4 3 2

This book is dedicated to
those couples
whose lives touched ours
to create
therapeutic changes

CONTENTS

FOREWORD

I have been impressed for a long time with Drs. Judith and Erich Cochés' contributions to the field of Group and Family Psychotherapy through their publications and presentations at meetings of the American Group Psychotherapy Association and other professional conferences. In *Couples Group Psychotherapy,* the Cochés' careful style, clinical sensitivity, scientific rigor and respect for structure is evident from cover to cover. The book clearly shows how the integration of these elements fosters effective treatment.

The reader soon becomes familiar with the basic concepts used by the authors in the development of their treatment design for working with couples in groups. Excellent clinical vignettes illustrate how the Cochés have evolved their approach and show what and how they have learned from critical treatment incidents during the process.

The companion videotape is a valuable teaching tool illustrating this approach. It includes a series of group vignettes with focus on a couple along with a follow-up session.

I found it easy to follow this well-documented program for group therapy with couples. The section describing the need for careful selection of couples and their preparation, the rationale for contracting for a close group experience, and the flexible and creative use of combined individual and family sessions is extremely meaningful and clear. The authors should be commended for placing strong emphasis on a careful diagnostic assessment preceding treatment and how it is helpful in outcome research. This is worthy of recognition in a field where treatment efficacy studies are rather limited.

We need to remember that there are no short cuts to becoming master therapists. The book demonstrates time and again how important it is to respect stages of individual and group development. I am impressed with the fact that the authors do not mean passive respect; in the discussion on the actual work with couples in groups (Chapter 4), the book presents strategies that are useful in fostering circular thinking, while teaching the couples basic concepts that underlie the group's philosophy and practice.

The book stresses the importance of careful planning in the selection of each exercise before it is introduced to the group. Structured interventions are neither trivial nor frivolous. They deepen and advance the learning gained in the unstructured part of the session. Whether original or taken from the literature, exercises which fit the dynamic process are a powerful tool.

The combination of non-directive and directive techniques in the two components of each session is rather ingenious and reflects the expertise and comfort of the authors in integrating several orientations and practices under a General Systems umbrella. As proposed in this volume, group and family therapy do not have to conflict or compete, but can be combined in a way that is logical, clinically astute, and therapeutically helpful to the patients.

For those who are afraid of problems of confidentiality when treating couples and families, I recommend reading carefully those parts of the book that deal with critical information emerging from either group, family or individual sessions. When one follows the authors' systemic thinking it is possible to understand how information flowing from one treatment modality to another can be safely used to greatly enhance the therapeutic experience. However, it requires a certain depth of clinical skill and sensitivity as postulated by the authors. This volume helps the reader achieve that depth.

The final section of the book takes the reader into further elaboration of their integrated theoretical model and the significance for couples treatment research. This is done with unusual clarity and congruence. What is at least equally important (should I say, perhaps, more enviable?) is that the Cochés communicate their ability to have creative fun while working effectively in the treatment of couples. The inscription in a book given to them is aptly stated: "We wish for you, in your marriage, many levels of creativity." Ditto from me!

ALBERTO SERRANO, M.D.
Professor of Psychiatry and Pediatrics
The University of Pennsylvania School of Medicine
Medical Director
Philadelphia Child Guidance Clinic

ACKNOWLEDGMENTS

Many years ago, in the first decade of our marriage, we began to realize that the happily-ever-after of the 1950s sit-coms didn't seem to apply to our friends, our colleagues, and ourselves. Back in the early ages of couples and group psychotherapy, little was discussed about coupling skills. Individuals were treated and illness was the model. We've come a long way, and we thank our many colleagues who have been mentors to us in one way or another. Special thanks go to four persons whose humanness has personally touched us: Carl Whitaker, Muriel Whitaker, James Bugental, and Olga Silverstein. Their ideas have been molded, adapted and integrated by us to our current gestalt.

Many thanks go to our publishing team: Danni Robinson, editorial assistant, who worked her way through many drafts and changes; Tamara Sucoloski, research assistant, whose knack at finding bibliographical data saved us from hours of searching; and Susan Rowland, administrative assistant, who has been tireless in keeping things organized. Long hours and tight deadlines did not faze these women.

A special thanks to Sharon Panulla, whose reading of an earlier version of the manuscript proved seminal in the current work. Natalie Gilman, our editor, and Mark Tracten, the publisher, remained calm and helpful in answering the countless concerns of the authors.

A final acknowledgment to our daughter, Juliette Laura Coché, who must often have felt some kind of kinship with these pages. We appreciate her patience with long working hours, and her assistance in organizing computer-printed pages.

INTRODUCTION

*Maybe that's why we are attracted to each other: I asked you,
you couldn't say no and I couldn't take it back.*

— *Ted*

For much of human history, marriage was considered a permanent, lifelong
bond between two people for the purposes of procreation and survival of the
family unit. In the Middle Ages, for example, marriages were frequently
arranged by the elders of the partners, for the betterment of their respective
families of origin.

Within the last century, the major thrust has shifted in the marital arena.
The shift has been away from procreation and survival as major determinants
of mate selection and bonding. Now the major goal of marriage for most
people is to derive personal satisfaction from the bond itself. This shift has
created confusion, fear, frustration, and competing models of marriage.

Maggie and Al had been married for 10 years before they discovered
that Maggie was in the marriage for life, while Al assumed that he would
leave should he "fall out of love." The two competing and very different
concepts of the marriage contract had never been discussed, and resulted
in rage, bewilderment, and a separation which was painful for both
partners, their families, and friends. It had simply never occurred to
them to discuss their basic assumptions about human partnership.

As long as the model of human partnership was basically survival, communication skills and passion were secondary in importance in the marital
hierarchy. Primary were consistency, responsibility, tenaciousness, and mutual
support of all family members. In *Fiddler on the Roof*, Tevya the milkman,
after 25 years of marriage, asks his wife if she loves him, only to find her
surprised and puzzled by the question. She finally gives him a list of all the
tasks she has done (washing his clothes, darning his socks, bearing his children)
and says incredulously, "If that's not love, what is?" thus expressing how alien
the other, more emotional concept of marriage is to her.

Today's model is much more complex. Since the goal is one of mutual
affection, mutual gratification, and the continuing *choice* of staying together,

marriage now requires a set of skills different from and more complex than those needed in the survival marriage. It becomes necessary that the inevitable abrasions and conflicts caused when two individuals bump up against one another be resolved adequately so that the couple can continue to be drawn voluntarily to one another. Basic skills in human communications, human sexuality, and interpersonal problem-solving, therefore, become essential to the welfare of the relationship. They become a kind of toolbox for marital longevity.

These skills are usually learned informally from one's elders, many of whom, however, had still entered marriage under the old contract or some variant thereof. When a child is born into a family, the early learnings in human communications give the child a basic set of interactional tools, which the child automatically carries into subsequent human interchanges. If the family was violent, or silent, or sneaky, or boisterous, or crude, it is only later in life that the child realizes that his family acted as a kind of universe for him, and that the way they handled human intimacy was problematic. By then, in adult years, the child will in some way or another have perpetuated the mistakes. It is then necessary to unlearn automatic styles of relating to others and learn new and more successful techniques.

Once an individual sets out to learn better relational skills, often motivated by the pain of lost relationships, abuse, anger, divorce, addictions, there is nowhere in the educational system to turn for guidance. There are no courses on human problem-solving in our school systems. Insurance companies will not support classes in emotional learning unless the learner carries the stigma of mental illness. Popular books teach cognitive principles, but do not give the personal guidance and follow-through necessary for the kind of change which is based on human experience as much as it is on human understanding. Books alone are simply insufficient.

Couples group psychotherapy provides both cognitive and experiential learning for couples. This multilevel learning enables men and women to resolve interpersonal conflicts and to keep the vibrancy in their relationship, hopefully with the result that the partners will continue to choose one another. The group narrows the gaping chasm that exists for many couples between their romanticized, Madison-Avenue expectations for a perfect marriage and a perfect spouse and their limited ability to achieve the wonderful marriage that they so long for.

Ideally, there would be a school for couples, a place where people could learn basic human interactive skills before joining together. Ideally, a partner could ask not only whether a mate is sexually safe for partnering, but also whether a potential partner has graduated from the school of human interaction and is emotionally ready to be a partner.

Despite a few attempts at an educational model, the vast majority of couples wait until one or both partners are disillusioned about the marriage and in some degree of human pain before seeking relief for their suffering. When they then come for help, much of the treatment process is one of reeducation, within a group setting, of skills mislearned in earlier family interactions.

THE PURPOSE OF THIS BOOK

This book teaches how to conduct group psychotherapy for couples. It teaches the reader how to conceptualize couples group psychotherapy, how to conduct the meetings, and how to incorporate this form of treatment into clinical practice.

In discussing couples group psychotherapy, the book presents a specific model which the authors developed in the course of the last five years. The model combines group psychotherapy techniques with marital therapy — an inclusive model of couples group psychotherapy. It provides theoretical and conceptual foundations from the fields of individual personality development, family systems theory, and group psychotherapy theory. It adapts the conceptual framework to the actual clinical application of the principles and research in these fields. It enables clinicians, through many and varied case examples, to transfer the application of the conceptual framework into actual treatment applications. It provides the clinician with a method of evaluating a group's success and the treatment outcome of the couples involved.

The model presented here necessitates prior knowledge and training in two separate but related clinical modalities: group psychotherapy in general and psychotherapy with couples and families. It is essential that at least one — and preferably both — of the group leaders conceptualize client change via the psychotherapy process in contextual terms. By this we mean that human change occurs within an interpersonal context and can, therefore, happen most efficiently when the psychotherapy process is conducted in a vibrant and interpersonal arena. This arena can be marital or family therapy, group therapy or — in the case of couples group psychotherapy — both couples and group psychotherapy simultaneously. What is central, in our opinion, is the assumption that it takes people to make people sick and people to make people well.

This model is a synthesis of two approaches which are brought together under the umbrella of General Systems Theory. While some of the conceptual origins come from the worlds of biology (von Bertalanffy, 1968) and social psychology (Lewin, 1951), their application in mental health services comes from two usually separate but not incompatible sectors: family therapy and group psychotherapy. We hope that this book is a contribution towards bringing these two worlds closer together.

During our clinical training in Europe and in the United States, we were frequently warned by our mentors against what we have come to call "seat-of-the-pants eclecticism" or "kitchen sink therapy." Nevertheless, we believe that it is legitimate and clinically wise to combine the schools of family therapy and group psychotherapy because they are conceptually compatible. A group sometimes operates like a family and a family has the properties of a group. Both are greater than the sum of their parts and the subsystems of each can be fully understood only through a knowledge of the working of the whole (Spitz, 1979).

The model has been developed in an outpatient setting, but is adaptable to varying populations and settings. It is cost effective, as is group psychotherapy for individuals who are not treated as part of a couple. It is time-efficient since considerable changes in the lives of a couple and their children are possible within fewer than 60 clinical hours. The power of the model rests on the combined skill of the leaders in family and in group psychotherapy. The purpose of the book is to infuse the reader with some of these skills as a part of training in systems therapy involving couples, families and groups.

This is a book for clinicians, as well as for clinicians in training, who are interested in becoming more skilled in working systemically with couples in a group format. It covers basic concepts in couples therapy and in group therapy only insofar as these concepts are germane to the treatment model presented in these pages. Thus, the book begins at the convergence of thought between these clinical worlds.

OVERVIEW OF THE BOOK

Couples Group Psychotherapy as presented here is a model of a closed-ended group in which four couples participate in a group which begins and terminates as a whole. The contract runs for 11 months, with two two-and-a-half hour sessions monthly. Strategies to set up these procedures and their rationales are presented in the appropriate chapters.

The book begins with the principles and concepts by which the model is structured. Part I describes how to structure a couples group. Chapter 1 discusses how to prepare potential couples for a couples group experience. Research on the value of good preparation for group psychotherapy is discussed together with clinical techniques needed to assess when to refer couples, how to answer questions and assist with resistance, and how to negotiate time and money issues. These explanations provide the clinician with the practical tools needed to form a group.

The first chapter also introduces the procedures used to assess strengths and weaknesses in a couple's relationship. These assessment procedures form the basis for goal setting for the couples at the beginning of the group and are used later in the clinical year to assess a couple's progress. They also lend themselves to ongoing clinical research if the therapists so choose.

Chapter 2 outlines the integration of couples group therapy into an overall treatment package for the individual, family, or couple who first request treatment. Once a decision has been made to have the couple participate in a couples group, the questions of how to maximize the therapeutic impact and how to integrate the group experience with adjunctive therapy outside the group must be addressed.

Chapter 3 discusses the policies which form the foundation of the structure of the couples groups in the authors' practice. These policies, developed over a five-year period, are presented together with their origins in group psychotherapy theory and research.

Part II presents concepts necessary for the treatment of couples in a group. Chapter 4 starts with concepts from the fields of marital and family therapy that form the foundation of our work with the couples. Chapter 5 discusses principles in building a cohesive working group, as these principles are adapted to a couples group model.

Chapter 6 follows the development of the group over time as it moves from its formation each fall as a newborn group with no common past history through the stages of development to an independently functioning group in the adult stage of group development. Chapter 7 introduces the structured interventions which we conduct in the second half of each session. Since they are not "prepackaged" but meant to be decided on in response to the group's mood and content, the chapter suggests methods by which meaningful learning experiences can be decided on in a short time.

Part III outlines the theoretical underpinnings of the practical suggestions made in prior chapters. Chapter 8 presents the cognitive map of the couples group psychotherapist, who decides how and when to intervene clinically at a given moment in time. It shows, in addition to the factors of group development and structure previously presented, how the therapist can target interventions at any one of four levels at any point in time. Deciding when to intervene at which level determines the power of the group for the leaders and members.

Chapter 9 then discusses the procedures necessary to maintain a fluid ongoing group from a structural standpoint. Handling of absences and lateness, fee collection, and physical structure of the group form the framework for ongoing clinical work. Recognizing and dealing effectively with emergencies also ensures that the structure of the group makes possible ongoing work for the members.

The final chapter presents an evaluative study which was designed to obtain the group participants' views of their couples groups: Which areas of their marital interactions improved? What was it about the group that appeared most effective to the members? The assessments and goals discussed in Chapter 1 form the anchoring points for this study.

The appendices present further details for carrying out the model clinically. Appendix A presents the actual assessment tools used in the group. Appendix B gives examples of the structured exercises used in the groups and in the concomitant workshops for the couples who are members of the groups. Appendix C contains the Group Psychotherapy Policies as they are used in all the therapy groups in the authors' practice.

The book has a companion training videotape, *Techniques in Couples Group Psychotherapy.* Four couples provided live group work to illustrate key concepts in video format. Some parts of the transcript have been integrated into those book sections which provide the conceptual framework for the techniques on the tape. We indicate those sections with a footnote on the page containing tape material. The names of the protagonists have been changed somewhat.

In summary, the parts of the book combine to form a model for clinical practice that we hope will add a new and valuable dimension to the effective treatment of couples.

---

*Available from Brunner/Mazel Publishers, 19 Union Square West, New York, NY 10003, (212) 924-3344.

PART I

Structuring Couples Group Psychotherapy

1.

Preparing Couples for Couples Group Psychotherapy

The hardest thing in a marriage is to be brave enough to open up about yourself, to take the risk that the person who listens to you will still love you.

—Nell

In the course of the last decade, more and more research and review articles have appeared in the group psychotherapy literature which demonstrate the importance of preparing prospective members for a group psychotherapy experience (Mayerson, 1984; Meadow, 1988; Richman, 1979). The consensus of these articles is that group members who have been adequately prepared for their therapy experience show more desirable group behaviors in the early stages of the group and get on with the therapeutic task much sooner than unprepared patients. Moreover, prepared groups become cohesive sooner and have fewer absences and dropouts (Roback & Smith, 1987).

Other advantages of preparation described in the literature will be pointed out later in this chapter. For now it may suffice to say that a solid and well thought-out preparation of the new member couple contributes greatly to the success of the complete group experience. It is quite similar to preparation for a sailing regatta. Inadequate preparation of the boat and getting off to a poor start frequently doom the hapless sailor to a much poorer showing than would have occurred otherwise.

Preparing couples for group psychotherapy is complex. First there is the problem of selection for the group, as well as that of creating a mix of couples who are likely to work well together. Then comes the preparation itself, including telling the new couple about the group and its likely effectiveness. Often there is resistance to group psychotherapy and this needs to be handled tactfully and effectively. This phase also includes the introduction to the group policies (see Chapter 3).

Another part of this preparation is what has been called "Role Induction" (Mayerson, 1984), meaning that the prospective group member is given a reasonably clear idea as to what is expected from a "good group member." In other words, the person is induced into the role of a cooperative, working group participant before the first group session.

The final focus of group therapy preparation is the assessment of the problem which the couple needs to work on. This is usually arrived at in a discussion between the couple and the therapist. A mutual agreement on the goals which the couple wants to reach is a vital beginning for later group processes and effective therapy work.

INVITING COUPLES TO JOIN A GROUP

Before preparing the couples for their group experience, the leaders have to determine which couples they want to invite into the group. A number of factors are worthy of consideration in putting together a new couples group. Among these are *motivation, homogeneity/heterogeneity,* and *match.*

Motivation

The couples entering a group may or may not be married and they may have varied motivations. For example, one couple joined the group because they wanted to marry but realized that their communication skills around key issues were so limited that marriage was unwise. They used the group for two years to build a foundation of basic skills in communicating anger, and in working with competitive struggles between them.

What is common to all prospective group members is a commitment to their relationship. There has to be an evident desire on the part of both partners to stay together and work things out when they hit a rough spot. Even though the couple may be in very serious trouble, neither partner has "one foot out the door." Each is not usually threatening the other with divorce or pushing the relationship to the brink of a breakup. In a few cases the couple may have been considering divorce but made an agreement with each other and with the group not to consider this option for the duration of the group year. Occasionally, the dynamics of a marriage are such that threats of divorce arise during the course of the group year. The projective blame syndrome and veiled threats are then dealt with therapeutically.

Erik's style of expressing intense loneliness and unrest was to somewhat flippantly and cavalierly suggest divorce as a weapon in a marital argument. When the couple first entered treatment, he suggested that they needed to move from their suburban home to a distant suburb which was physically close to his mother. When Nan begged to stay at the home she cherished, Erik angrily stated that divorce might be necessary if they could not relocate as a pair.

Reluctantly and with depression mounting in severity, Nan "succumbed" to what she believed to be her fate. The couple relocated. Nan became more withdrawn into her business and came home to the distant suburbs later each evening as the weeks progressed.

When the couple, in a desperate attempt to learn to negotiate, decided to join the couples group, they also agreed to give up threats of divorce as a marital weapon. Since neither partner wanted a divorce, the affirmative stance vis à vis the marriage acted as a strategic intervention in and of itself.

Heterogeneity/Homogeneity of Members in a Group

The couples groups are heterogeneous in relation to the members' age, diagnosis, and severity of marital problem. We have formed groups which included people as old as 75 and as young as 25. When there is a large age spread, some remarkable, therapeutically useful transference phenomena occur in which the older people relate to the other couples as they might relate to their adult children, while the younger couples get into various aging-parents issues with the older folks.

We also prefer groups with variations in the severity of marital problem and/or individual diagnosis. Some couples believe that their marriage is fundamentally solid but that "the spark has gone out of the relationship"; they choose to participate in the group in order to enhance and revitalize the marital foundation. Other members are going through a very serious crisis and actually look at the group as their "last hope." Many have been in marriage therapy before but were unsuccessful. Having both types of couples in the group is encouraging for both: Those with the serious problem find much to learn from the others, while the latter are relieved to learn that they are "not so bad off" as their peers in the group or as they had thought.

In addition to receiving the couples assessment, members of the group are also given individual assessment tools and are assigned a DSM-III-R diagnosis. This is necessary for insurance purposes, but also aids the therapist in determining intervention strategies. This can be done without losing sight of the systems aspects of the work at hand.

Frequent diagnoses are personality disorders, neuroses, learning disabilities in adults, and adjustment disorders. Many clients enter a group with a mild to moderate form of depression, quite a few suffer from serious depression, and many have addictive disorders. We do not invite anyone with an overt psychosis, but we have on a few occasions had one or two persons with a borderline diagnosis. We find that these clients require more alertness on the part of the therapists, but they can do well overall in the group if the leadership is skillful.

Ted seemed to be of below average intelligence. He stammered, fumbled for words, spoke softly, and spent so much time in his own thoughts that he seemed both absent and vacant to many members of the world-at-large. The youngest of six children, raised by a single mother, Ted lacked parental models of self-confidence and assertiveness. He actually performed above average on the intelligence tests given to him when he entered treatment.

Although a learning disability was suspected, testing revealed that the dysfunction was primarily one of self-esteem and of ego development. Ted functioned like an innocent child in a big and heartless world. Within himself, an active and violent fantasy world existed in which long hours were spent plotting revenge for the inequities inflicted on him by others.

Ted's wife, Georgia, was the daughter of a wealthy, refined family. Her father, a pharmacist, was multiply addicted to sleeping medications (to knock him out) and amphetamines (to wake him up). Georgia learned quite early to protect her family, especially her father, so as to protect the family secret. Her "cover-up" ability was superb when she married Ted. The marriage was "problem free" when they entered couples therapy, according to them. When Ted withdrew into his violent fantasy world, Georgia covered for him publicly through her wit and charm. When Ted's hostility was directed against Georgia, she either joked him out of it or withdrew in fear. The couple was entirely unable to address the issues in the marriage at the start of the couples group. We, as leaders, were watchful that Ted be neither protected by the group nor scapegoated. He was a prime candidate for either position.

Members joining a group will have different levels of prior experience in a group. Some of the couples are likely to be "returners" who had participated in a couples group previously and are signing on for a second or, occasionally, a third 11-month round. In other couples, one partner may have been in a prior group experience of a different kind. Finally, some members are likely to be completely new to group psychotherapy. It is particularly with these latter clients that pre-group preparation is of paramount importance, since pre-group anxiety is likely to be highest in inexperienced group participants.

The one area in which we plan homogeneity is what is sometimes called "cognitive homogeneity." We try to put couples together who are somewhat similar in intellectual and cognitive functioning.

Cognitively, members are average or above average in intellectual function-ing and have a variety of "cognitive styles," that is, ways of organizing their experience to form their own definition of interpersonal reality. Some mem-bers are gifted in warm, nurturing ways of thinking about others, while others may be cool and distant, yet insightful and incisive. Some members are very concrete and matter-of-fact, while others are facile in thinking psychodynamically, systemically, or metaphorically. Some are remarkably articulate, while others have great difficulty in knowing and/or expressing how they feel. Most members appreciate humor and enjoy the laughter which is central to the fluidity of group functioning.

In our groups all members are expected to meet certain membership criteria as listed on a sheet describing the group which is given to prospective members and referring therapists:

1. An intimate relationship of at least three years duration with the current partner.

2. Marital or couple problems for which solutions have been attempted with insufficiently satisfying results.

3. Ongoing or previous individual, couples, or family psychotherapy with one of the group leaders or elsewhere.

4. An interest in learning from and participating with other adults.

5. An intense desire to improve the intimacy and mutual satisfaction in the relationship.

The Matching Process in Group Formation

When a couples group is being formed, it is most advisable for the thera-pists to think of two couples with strong relationship skills who can function as the "core group." We then choose two additional couples to round out the group who are likely to work well with the core group. This choice can be on the basis of similarity of marital issues, such as addictions or illness.

We have found that four couples is the ideal size for the group. We have run groups with five couples and with three couples only to find that the groups did not work as well: With five couples, some people have complained about insufficient time spent on their issues; with three couples, there are not enough people to work up an active give and take and lively exchange of ideas.

Placing couples together can also be done on the basis of intergenerational issues: A couple who have lost a child may work well with a couple who have no family of origin nearby. Often, quieter couples are mixed with livelier couples, dual-career couples with those in more traditional roles, urbanites with suburban couples. This kind of variety adds tension and drama as couples learn to be close to people they used to think of as very different in terms of life style, socioeconomic status, or ethnic heritage. Later on, as cohesiveness develops, one hears comments like: "When I first met you I thought I could never feel close to you; now I feel more at home with you than I do with my own family." The universality of being coupled and of being a person forms the glue in the diversity of selection.

Inclusion can also be on the basis of wanting to avoid the "solo outsider." The concept of the solo outsider states that it is very strenuous for a group to contain a member with a trait which is quite extreme and sets him/her apart from the rest of the group. For example, if the group contains only one person with an addiction, one might find that the rest of the group does not show as much understanding for this person's plight as one would wish. It is better for the group to have at least one other person with a similar problem. The same goes for significant differences in age or severity of diagnosis (e.g., depression).

At times, it is unavoidable to have a solo outsider in the group. Gerry was the only learning disabled adult in his group. With some sensitivity and guidance from the therapist, the group can be helped to deal with such differences constructively. However, if such situations are not handled well, the "outsider" is in some danger of becoming the group's scapegoat.

THE SCREENING INTERVIEW: MUTUAL DECISION MAKING

Preparing a couple for group psychotherapy is accomplished in a variety of ways (Mayerson, 1984; Nichols, 1976). Sometimes, couples watch a demonstration tape of a couples group at work or talk with current group members whom they happen to know. And they may receive a booklet of instructions on how to be a "good group participant." Some therapists prefer to do their group psychotherapy preparation in small groups, others in special meetings with the prospective individual or couple. We generally use the latter approach.

Goals of Couples Group Preparation

Our preparatory meetings have a number of goals: Changing the "frame" or the way a couple thinks of changing, sparking enthusiasm, explaining boundaries, and inducing effective group behaviors.

Changing the Frame for Change

This seemingly confusing phrase is actually a concept which is most often found in the literature on Strategic Family Therapy (Keeney & Ross, 1985). Many of the changes which people are able to make in psychotherapy are actually a product of seeing the world a bit differently than before they entered therapy. The field of cognitive behavior therapy (Beck, 1979) uses this way of understanding change, and discusses the power of one's world view in influencing the way we behave, think, and feel towards ourselves and towards someone else.

The same concept applies to group therapy. Most couples are embarrassed to speak of their problems in front of anyone else, even with a therapist, when they enter therapy. The problems of the marriage or in the individuals in the marriage are a source of shame, and the idea of sharing them with a group of strangers sounds anything but therapeutic. Until couples come to understand that they stand to gain both an emotionally gratifying experience and effective treatment at a modest price from their participation in a group, they are unlikely to be willing to even consider the option. Therefore, the first way in which a couple must be prepared for a group is to accept the value of a group. Only when psychotherapy ceases to be something to be ashamed of can a couple begin to accept working in a group.

Sparking Enthusiasm

This aspect of group psychotherapy preparation may be seen as "selling the group" to the new couple. Many couples have to overcome tremendous hesitation and fear before they even come for marital therapy. The idea of a group is even more frightening to them and can approach a level of terror for one of the partners. Frequently, couples question, for example, how a group can be more effective than marital therapy sessions in which the therapist's full attention is devoted to one couple alone.

At this point, it becomes important for us not only to impart information about the many advantages of group psychotherapy (learning from other couples, empathy, mutual caring, etc.) but also to communicate our genuine belief in the group and enthusiasm for it. If the therapist enjoys being in the group and finds that the couples who complete it are more loving and more satisfied in their relationships due to the group's effect, it will become apparent to the new couple and may well spark the enthusiasm which overcomes their hesitation.

In this process, understanding the fantasies of the future group member about what goes on in a psychotherapy group becomes very important. Most people have some preconceived notions about group psychotherapy, frequently derived from the mass media. These notions may have given rise to fears and hesitations. Some people imagine that the group is one continuous ordeal of hard, insistent confrontation (as shown in some shows about drug treatment), while others picture a collection of oddballs (as they may have seen in a situation comedy) in which the couple would be the only sane people there. It is very important to have a sense of what the pertinent resistance fantasies are so that the therapist can deal with the fears and can correct the misconceptions as much as possible.

Dealing With Resistance

The best way to deal with therapeutic resistance is to begin with the language of the therapist. If resistance implies doing something which is counter to someone's judgment, hesitancy implies moving carefully and slowly. If "denial" implies overlooking something which is obvious, caution implies taking care of what exists. Thus, it becomes obvious that any couple in their right (collective) mind would be hesitant of any commitment of 11 months which could harm as well as help their marriage. It also becomes obvious that a couple experiencing active distress would be cautious about further disturbing a rocky status quo. If the therapist puts him or herself in the shoes of the client couple, it becomes much easier to identify with what that couple needs:

1. Clarity about the expectations and procedures of the group.
2. Guidance in choosing to be a member without feeling railroaded.
3. Reassurance that the group will act as a "safe harbor" for the couple's pain, and as a catalyst for fruitful change.

When preparing a couple for a group, we suggest that the therapist avoid any surprises until the group takes over. Therefore, we suggest that questions be answered honestly, and that cautiousness and hesitancy be treated with respect. Guidance in how to benefit from the group is very valuable. Since couples have no idea about what they are about to experience, it is very useful for them to hear about who the other couples are, how old they are, which topics will be covered, and other basic information about the group.

Psychological resistance is *always* mutual, although it may seem implanted in one partner or the other. Frequently, the male carries the resistance for the couple. As Nate says, "It pains me to say that, but I also must confess that I really did not want to come to group therapy. I was kind of holding onto the door frame out there as Lee dragged me in here for the first session."

Respectful inquiry into the nature of the hesitancy, analysis of the function of the hesitancy for the couple, and patient guidance thorough strategically placed clinical interventions enables a couple to tip the balance of the stability/change scale towards the "change" vector.

Karl and Randy were very smart people. Karl, at the youthful age of 24, landed a job as a journalist for a prestigious periodical. Randy graduated from "one of the Ivies" before she turned 20. While Randy was enthusiastic about the prospect of being in a group, Karl came equipped with honest reporter-like questions involving therapist credentials, the validity of group therapy, the bad press about group therapy, the expected outcome of group therapy, and research reviews. Accepting his questions as legitimate and consistent with his highly cognitive and questioning posture towards feelings of sexual intimacy, we invited him to read professional literature about group therapy and supplied him with the necessary reprints. The couple benefitted tremendously from their two years in the group.

Role Induction

Role induction is the process of informing prospective group members about the expected behaviors in group therapy. In signing up new members for a couples group, one may assume that these people are disadvantaged because they know very little about how they should act or be and what kind of interactions are considered desirable in a group (Nichols, 1976). Without this knowledge, people will guess. They may thus treat the group like a kaffeeklatsch, a board meeting, or a religious revival group, depending on which analogy they believe fits best. Or they may have read about group therapy in the media and try to behave according to what they saw there. Even some people who have been in group psychotherapy before may not necessarily interact in a way which fits the couples group. For them, too, some role induction is a good idea.

Teaching desirable group behaviors   Certain behaviors are likely to pay off handsomely for the group member and are therefore worth teaching. The two most important within-group behaviors are self-disclosure and interpersonal feedback.

Self-disclosure   Research during the last two decades has shown that for nonpsychotic group therapy clients the positive therapeutic effect of their group experience depends in large part on their own willingness to self-disclose (Coché & Dies, 1981). There are some depressed patients who may get some benefit from being helpful to others without a high degree of self-disclosing, but they are the exception. For most clients, the old rule stands: Your group therapy success depends on your degree of openness to the others in the group.

It is valuable to explain to the new group members that basically there are two kinds of self-disclosure in groups. One is telling the group about your life situation, about your background, your marriage, etc. The other is of the here-and-now kind; letting the group know how you feel at this moment. If you are feeling nervous about being here, angry, joyful, etc., let the group know about it.

Interpersonal feedback   The new group participant is encouraged to give other group members feedback on their behaviors. It is worthwhile to explain to new members what is meant by this and how they might proceed.

There is some debate as to when this is best done: Some therapists prefer to have the group get underway and then give instructions for constructive feedback, while others see it as an integral part of group member preparation.

In teaching new members about feedback it is advisable to spend some time on it and explain it in detail early in the group life. The client is taught to report to others about his/her emotional reaction to their behaviors. What is central is that it is the self-disclosure of a feeling which arose in response to something the other person did. An example would be a comment like: "When you talk to your wife like that, I feel . . . ."

It is especially important that the client understand that the feedback should be nonjudgmental even though feeling-laden. If words like "mean," "terrible," "obnoxious" are used, the feedback giver is already judging. Such judgments are sure to produce defensiveness and undermine the value of the feedback. Feedback which is nonjudgmental and feeling-oriented gives the recipient of the feedback the information needed to consider doing something about the behavior in question. Change may be in order because one is concerned about the reaction one has caused in others or else one may choose to keep the behavior and accept the reaction as the "price to pay" for it. The fact that one has choices in the responses to feedback makes it less threatening to the newcomer to group psychotherapy.

Creating Expectations for Successful Membership

These explanations of self-disclosure and feedback take some of the mystique out of the group psychotherapy process, which then begins to seem to the client like something he/she will be able to master. The client begins to expect that he/she can be a successful group member and can be acceptable to the others in the group.

Having generated this expectation of success, the therapist also communicates the expectation of a successful outcome. We often discuss with the couple which goals are reasonable and which are not, thus providing some guidance in setting expectations which are positive, optimistic, and reasonably attainable.

Preparing a Foundation for Later Group Cohesiveness

As is known from the research (France & Dugo, 1985; Mayerson, 1984; Roback & Smith, 1987), well-prepared groups have fewer member absences and fewer dropouts. By being more consistent in their attendance, members communicate to each other that the group is important to them and that they will go out of their way to attend. This spirit creates a more cohesive group climate and thus permits the group to move into the working phase more swiftly and smoothly.

ASSESSMENT

Assessment of a couple's problem begins long before a couple are considered for group participation. It actually begins with the first phone call and continues through the marital therapy sessions thereafter. The therapists form hypotheses about the way in which the partners function with each other and with their families, how their balance of power works, and the methods they employ to avoid intimacy. In the interviews with the couple, the therapist also learns about the techniques the partners have used so far to deal with their problems and about the results obtained with these strategies. Finally, an evaluation is made whether it is appropriate for this couple to join the group.

Once a couple are invited to join a group, a more formal assessment procedure is added to the interviews done so far. The partners complete two measures designed to provide the therapists with additional diagnostic information: the Couples Assessment Inventory and the Symptom Checklist (SCL-90 or SCL-90-R). The Couples Assessment Inventory appears in the appendix. The SCL-90-R is available from Clinical Psychometric Research, Inc., P.O. Box 619, Riderwood, MD 21139. This chapter will discuss the two measures which are being used, the rationale for pregroup diagnostic assessment, and some other possible instruments worthy of consideration.

The Couples Assessment Inventory (Appendix A-1)

This instrument was designed and evaluated by the authors. It was not intended to be a psychological test in the strict sense of the word, but was meant as a source of information for the therapists and a stimulus for inducing circularity of thinking and for discussion between the two partners. As indicated by the instructions, we request that the couple spend an hour discussing the issues together after each partner spends about 45 minutes filling out the form by him/herself.

The first question in the Inventory explores the qualities that attracted a person to his/her spouse and asks how these qualities have changed with time. Though this usually encourages partners to say "nice" things about each other, some rather acerbic remarks about how these qualities have developed over time are not uncommon. When each partner reflects on his/her reaction to the partners' attractive qualities, a systems perspective is introduced, revealing how each quality provokes a reaction which can, in turn, enhance or stifle this quality in the partner. Thus, a husband may find that through his reactions (for example, criticism of her lack of seriousness) he may have diminished exactly those qualities (such as fun-lovingness) which had initially attracted him to his wife.

The second question elicits the problems in the marriage as seen by each partner, clarifies the problems, and provides data on each partner's view of "who owns the problem." We ask: Does this person see him/herself as the source of the problem, does he/she blame the partner or is the problem seen as a relationship issue? The degree of blaming demonstrated here often gives the therapists a glimpse of how resistant the couple will be to working together in a nonblaming way. As stated before, until a couple can move beyond mutual blame, marriages (and groups) will remain stuck.

The third question furthers the idea that change will reside in each individual and in the couple. As a person reflects on personal goals, the therapeutic change a person desires becomes clearer. In addition, the respondent becomes aware that every personal change will also affect the relationship.

The last two questions on the Assessment Form ask about the parents' marriage, thereby creating an intergenerational mind set — an awareness of the relationship between a couple's problem and issues in each parents' marriage. A discussion of this question thus predisposes the couple to intergenerational work in the group.

Couples who choose to do a thorough job completing the Assessment Inventory find that it is a time-consuming but rewarding task. It stimulates discussions, has obvious face validity, and can propel a couple in a systemic therapeutic direction. Of course, not everyone chooses to spend a good deal of time on the task. Some people give only very cursory responses and — as we have found out, at times — not all the ensuing discussions are constructive. Thus, a couple caught in mutual blame is usually unable to benefit from or tolerate a discussion of the questionnaire.

Couples are asked to work on the form between the first and second sessions and to be ready for a discussion of their responses in the second session. In that session, the clients themselves read excerpts from their forms and discuss their answers to the degree to which they choose to divulge the material. Since this is only the second group session, it is understandable when someone is not ready to disclose all the data from the Assessment Form. However, most couples are willing to get moving towards their goal and are, therefore, prepared to share their responses with the group. In fact, many show a surprising frankness which helps to create an expectation that self-disclosure is the order of the day. This, in turn, contributes to the development of cohesiveness.

In the following transcript, three couples give us their responses to the questionnaire, in terms of what each wanted when they joined the group.*

JMC: Let's review what each of you wanted when you first joined the group. Lee, can you tell us what the problem was with you and Nate, when you first joined?

Lee: Yeah. We couldn't resolve conflicts. Every time we had a fight over

---

*Transcript from the videotape, *Techniques in Couples Group Psychotherapy.*

something or a problem came up in which we both got angry, I would calm down and want to make peace before Nate did. And he would stay angry. And so we wouldn't be able to deal with the problem and this tense silence would last for hours or days. And then the issue itself would just get pushed under the rug. We both wanted to get married, but I was really afraid to marry somebody when we didn't have the skills to resolve conflicts.

JMC: Nate, how did you see it?

Nate: Yeah, it's fairly accurate what she says.

JMC: Gerry, do you remember how you first introduced yourself to the group?

Gerry: Yes, I said, "Hello, my name is Gerry and I can't spell." I had a terrible time all through school. I couldn't spell and I went to great lengths to try to hide that problem. I felt that I was stupid. And then, when Dale asked me to join her here in therapy, I felt as though I was throwing myself a rope. And then when you, Judy, suggested I take some testing, then finding out that I did have a learning disability, for the first time in 28 years I felt that I wasn't stupid.

JMC: Dale, how did this affect your marriage?

Dale: Because Gerry felt so awful about himself, I felt as though I had to protect him. Especially when it came to conflict. I had a lot of trouble telling him when I had a problem with something he was doing, because I felt sorry for him. I didn't want to make him feel worse about himself. And by the time we came to therapy, we were really ready to change that pattern.

Will and Denise expressed their goal like this:

Will: When we first came in, we were concerned that the marriage was getting very stale and that things weren't working out very well. As we got deeper into the marriage, with pressures of graduate school, with working, we just weren't having the kind of fun and excitement that we did when we were dating. And it seemed to take place just about the time . . . , just after we got married.

Denise: Yeah, well, I entered the marriage having learned from my parents that once you get married, that was it. You were committed. All you had . . . It was work. You had to have . . . just work on the marriage constantly . . . and children definitely made it worse.

In one session Judith reviewed their questionnaire responses with Erik and Nan:

JMC: Erik and Nan, let's focus on you. Take out your initial questionnaire and lets go through the questions on it. First, Nan, tell us the qualities

which motivated you to choose Erik and then tell us how these qualities have withstood the test of time.

Nan: What I wrote was "intelligent and talented and he still is, but he doesn't
share it with me. And he's cheerful and considerate and he still is, but
not to me."

JMC: Erik, how about you?

Erik: I saw Nan as strong and decisive. When I joined the group, I wrote, "I
no longer see her that way. I saw her as kind and well meaning. She still
is, but I think it's naive. I thought she was very intelligent, but I'm
really not sure about that anymore."

Nan: (reading from her assessment inventory): "The major problem from
my point of view is the triangle going on," I wrote, "between Erik, his
mother, and me. He excludes me and if it's a question between his
family and the two of us, the choice is always his family. Oh, we've tried
talking about it. Nothing changes. It seems like we understand each
other less and less the more we talk about it."

JMC: Nan, finally, can you tell us how you are determined to make your
marriage different from that of your parents?

Nan: (reading from her assessment inventory): "In my family . . . in my
parent's marriage, no one ever discussed feelings. The bad ones were
just not allowed to exist and that has caused me some terrible problems.
And I don't want our marriage to be that way."

The Symptom Checklist (SCL-90-R)

The SCL-90-R, which was developed by Leonard Derogatis, is a list of 90
symptoms, ranging from headaches to crying spells. The client rates each
symptom according to the degree to which it has been troublesome in the last
two weeks. Each symptom is either absent (rated 0) or present to a severity
ranging from 1 to 4. The test is then computer-scored and produces standard
scores on nine clinical categories and three summation categories.

The SCL-90-R usually takes only about 10 to 20 minutes. Participants have
few quarrels with it. Because it asks for the presence of symptoms, it has face
validity and clients are reassured to know that we want to know each
individual's personal level of distress. This knowledge reduces the client's
inevitable anxiety that he/she might get "lost" to the therapist in a sea
of couples.

At some time before or after the second session, one of the therapists meets
with each couple and gives the partners feedback on their SCL-90-R profile.
Most couples appreciate the time and effort taken, even if the outcome
presents disturbing material or little that is new. If either denial or a plea for
help (which may appear like an exaggeration of the distress) are evident,
these issues can be brought up in the feedback session and suggestions for

their therapeutic handling can be discussed. Usually, couples are also interested in having this discussion of the assessment data continued in the group because they find that the experience focuses their attention on their work for the future.

WHY DO ASSESSMENTS?

1. Assessment Provides Additional Diagnostic Input

Careful diagnosis before inviting a couple to join the group has been found to be very important in preventing later calamities (Spitz, 1979). Not infrequently, a couple will present itself quite differently on paper than it did in the initial pregroup interview or even in its couples therapy sessions before the group. Having the assessment data is analogous to receiving an outside consultation from a trusted clinician. One may discover unforeseen trouble spots or hidden strengths. At the very least, one receives a confirmation of one's prior impressions and can share these impressions with the clients themselves.

2. The Assessment Provides a View of the Defensive Structure

The assessment data, especially the SCL-90-R, can provide glimpses not only of the depth of despair but also of the degree of denial.

Leslie had been in couples psychotherapy for quite a while, spending much effort in trying to convince the therapist that her whole problem was her husband, Morris, who in turn was equally convinced that Leslie's behavior was the problem. The SCL-90-R profile showed that the denial, especially on Leslie's part, was quite serious. Despite her obvious discomfort and unhappiness, she had marked most symptoms as absent. This outcome, together with mostly bland and blaming responses on the Couples Assessment Inventory, served as a warning to the therapists that Morris and Leslie would be very resistant to change.

3. Assessments Assist in Goal Setting

The Couples Assessment Inventory, in particular, pushes the couple to think of the problem in very specific terms and in ways which conceptualize it as solvable and systemic. Members are encouraged to think about the reciprocity involved in those marital processes which cause them unhappiness rather than blaming each other. They often derive hope and encouragement from getting away from the blame pattern. Thus, early in the development of the group, the Assessment Form enhances the motivation to stop denying and go to work on the issues.

4. Assessment Lays the Foundation for Treatment Evaluation

If at any point later on in the group the therapists or the clients want to know how far a couple have come, we can refer to the initial Assessment Form. We can then ask the couple how they see these issues now. This is done more or less routinely in the termination phase of the group when the couple has to decide whether or not to sign up for another year. When appropriate, we can also give the partners another SCL-90-R to see how they are feeling at a later time. This provides data on how much the couple have progressed and how much more therapy is indicated. Here, too, surprises are possible and it may be advisable to have written input.

WORKABLE ASSESSMENT PROCEDURES

The therapist wishing to institute assessment as part of a group therapy program has a wide variety of instruments available. In selecting these and administering them to the clients, the therapist should follow a few procedural rules.

1. Keep it Simple

At an early phase, when the motivation to participate in a group is still somewhat shaky, it is not wise to push the clients to take a large test battery. This would in all likelihood increase resistance and turn people off when they most need encouragement. Naturally, by being brief in the test battery that is presented, one incurs some loss in the solidity of the data. An MMPI is likely to produce more powerful results than an SCL-90-R, but it might also increase the resistance.

2. Keep in Mind the Value of Face Validity

For a new group member to be confronted by a test which makes no sense or seems to have no relation to the tasks at hand is a very discouraging and antagonizing experience. Seeing that the instrument given relates directly to couples issues and to one's personal unhappiness motivates the client to fill out the form and to bring it in and share the results with others.

3. Give Focused and Timely Feedback

Another strategy to enhance people's motivation is to give the testing feedback early on. The scoring should be done expeditiously and an oral report given to the couple as soon as possible. The feedback session itself can be used to bring the couple's goals for the treatment into sharper focus so as to reduce resistance and denial and to enhance the partners' optimism that their efforts towards reading the goal are worthwhile and have a reasonable chance to be successful.

Erich's feedback to Erik and Nan sounded like this:*

> Erik, for someone who did not want to be in the group your test results look somewhat unsettling. There is a severe elevation in the depression score, showing mostly symptoms of unhappiness, guilt, and a feeling of being trapped. For you, Nan, it showed a generally high level of distress, with elevations mostly in depression, anxiety, and anger.

4. Choose Tools Which are Therapeutically Consistent

The tests chosen as assessment tools should be consistent with the therapists' theoretical position. The Couples Assessment Inventory helps us because it is systemically oriented to begin with. The SCL-90-R, though much more person-focused, at least does not contradict our philosophy and the approach we take in the feedback session is very much geared towards helping the couple in integrating the findings into their work as a couple and in the group.

---

*Transcript from the videotape, *Techniques in Couples Group Psychotherapy*.

2.

Structuring an Efficient Treatment Package

Please, say it one more time and let me see if I can block it out one more time.

—Morris to Leslie

COUPLES GROUP OVERVIEW

Once a couple are prepared to join a group, as well as to participate in individual, couples, or family therapy once every three weeks or more throughout the life of the group, the couple have agreed to a structure which will enable changes to happen in the relationship with themselves, each other, the therapists involved, and a number of couples they have yet to meet.

The agreement to become part of this community of couples is a bit like beginning regular, rhythmic, aerobic exercise when one begins a weight-loss program. While there are countless diets on the market, nothing assures success more than a combined and regular approach to physical exercise as part of an approach to healthy living. Similarly, couples therapy comes in many formats.

We have chosen a slow, steady approach to change which approaches the task from many levels and involves multiple therapy experiences. Each experience is designed to maximize the invitation to constructive change and to minimize travel time, inconvenience to the consumer or client, and cost. By assuring two group meetings of over two hours each, and interspersing therapy time devoted only to the members of a particular nuclear family or couple, we have designed a package which is able to "catch" therapy issues before they fade or become mishandled. In this chapter we present an overview of the steps in designing an efficient treatment package. In later chapters we look at some of the ingredients in closer detail.

From talking with colleagues and from our knowledge of the literature, we have come to the conclusion that the "usual" group meets weekly for one and one-half hours and is "open-ended," meaning that new members enter the group as others leave it and "make room" for the newcomer (Kluge, 1974). Though this appears to be the most common group psychotherapy model, it is not the only one and not necessarily the most efficient depending on the goals one has for the members. In this chapter, we will present a very different group structure, together with the rationale for its various ingredients and the experiences we have gathered with it so far.

We chose a group structure of twice-monthly sessions of two and one-half hours each, framed in an 11-month closed-ended experience, which means that all participants begin and end their group therapy experience together.

Complete Closed-Group Experience

The couples who sign up for the group agree to stay with it for the full 11-month duration. They will have two sessions each month, a total of 22 sessions. Their sessions are usually biweekly, but occasionally there are three-week spans between sessions, depending on the number of certain weekdays in a month and holidays.

The major reason for this approach is that closed-ended groups have a better chance to experience group developmental stages together. All group members have to conquer the typical anxiety felt in a group in its beginning stage; together they go through the growth phases of dependence and counter-dependence towards the leaders; they struggle with their issues of interdependence, intimacy, and honesty as a unit; finally they all face the termination of the group. All these stages provide opportunities for personal growth and learning. Working through these stages together is a bit like going through the stages of life; it creates a more intense group experience than can be obtained in a comparable open-ended group.

The necessity for members to develop all group phases together generates an opportunity to feel communality with others not merely on the basis of outside characteristics (such as similarity in age or marital problem) but also on the basis of shared here-and-now experiences. People feel a bond with others because they are going through a group crisis together, solving problems together, and feeling similar feelings at the same time. The shared joy, fear, sadness, loathing, and laughter creates a kind of universality which is in many ways superior to the kind one experiences upon finding that others are also having problems with depression or substance abuse (Rutan & Stone, 1984).

In his listing of the "curative factors" of group psychotherapy, Yalom (1975) describes the factor of "Universality" in some detail. It is the kind of comfort felt by group members upon finding that other members are struggling with similar problems. It often helps the client, especially in the early stages of group participation, to feel less alone and less ashamed of having a problem which heretofore one had thought of as unique. This can frequently encourage the client new to groups to self-disclose more and thus to enhance therapeutic benefit.

Having closed groups may seem inconvenient to prospective couples. Some want to start in a group right away. Others may believe that the problem which prompted them to seek marital therapy is less serious by the time the group is ready to start. As a result, there is a certain degree of loss because the couples' timing is "off." Yet, once a couple is convinced of the potential value of the group by the therapist or by former group members who praised it, couples are usually willing to wait until the beginning of the next group round and become group participants then.

Twice-Monthly, Longer Sessions

Psychotherapy is a consumer service. Our couples lead busy lives and must deal with business trips, baby-sitters, fatigue at a day's end, and other problems that make weekly appointments difficult to keep. The model of less frequent but longer sessions was originally created merely for our consumers' convenience. We know that many couples who lead full lives find it much more manageable to commit to two evenings per month for a year. It feels more like a time-out together rather than a weekly chore.

When we instituted the new pattern a few years ago, two unforeseen psychological advantages emerged serendipitously. First, the sessions seemed even greater in intensity than in the weekly groups; in the two and one-half hours available, couples were able to delve into matters in much greater depth than they did in a one-and-a-half-hour session. Second, the time span between sessions actually gave couples more opportunity to work on matters on their own between sessions. They could and did try out new behaviors, perform therapeutic homework assignments, and try to work out disagreements. Many sessions open with reports on what was accomplished between sessions, with a genuine sense of accomplishment by the couple, as if to say, "Look at what we did without you." As far as we are concerned, so much the better.

At times the reports are less glowing. One assignment, given to Erik and Nan, was not completed to the satisfaction of the group*:

JC: Erik and Nan, about a month ago I asked you whether you would be able to have at least one dinner a week without Erik's mother. Can you tell the group how it's going?

---

*Transcript from the videotape, *Techniques in Couples Group Therapy.*

Nan: Can I start? Well, not too well. Um, we have managed to do it a couple of times, maybe three or four by now.

JC: In total, or per week?

Nan: In total. Um...

Nate: And how many weeks ago was the assignment?

Nan: This was about three months, I guess? Um, I push for it. Erik really does have trouble doing it. I know he does. And when we go it's very nice. I have a wonderful time. I can even sometimes forget that Erik is pretty uncomfortable with it. Not with me, but with being away from his mother, and leaving her alone. Ah, last week, I very much wanted to go out on a Friday night, Erik just couldn't do it.

Erik: Well, we went out Wednesday and Thursday and we were going to be out again on Saturday and Sunday.

Nan: Right ... but the next Tuesday and Wednesday...

Will: I thought this was supposed to be like a date? Like one date a week.

Erik: There's only seven nights in the week too, and ah...

JC: This group is incredulous.

Split Sessions

The increased depth noted by therapists and patients alike was also achieved through the splitting of the sessions into the unstructured and structured portions.

First half: Unstructured couples group psychotherapy During the first half of an evening's session, the floor is open to anyone. The couples know this, plan ahead, and raise their own issues without delay. They bring up whatever pressing problem has arisen or they give a follow-up report on something which had been worked on in previous sessions. Some couples "save" a hot topic for the safety of the group.

> Karl and Randy had been living together for three years when they entered the couples group. In the third year of living together, their sexual activity had diminished and ultimately stopped completely. Because of their respective backgrounds and sexual histories, they were unable to even talk about their sexual difficulties when alone with each other. After some time in the group, however, they were able to raise the issue in therapy.
> The other group members offered them expertise, reassurance, and support. As a result, the group became a "safe harbor" in which much needed work in human intimacy could take place.

Usually a natural flow develops; one couple may open up with a problem which is currently "hot" and the others chime in with observations on the dynamics in this couple, with feedback on the partners' behaviors, or with experiences of their own on similar issues. There is a fluidity, an easy give and take. As a specific couple's problem has been dealt with, another couple may raise an issue in their marriage, or a particular couple's problem may expand into a more general group discussion of the underlying issue.

> Karl and Randy were in a group with Will and Denise, a couple whose sexual adventures stopped cold upon the slipping of the wedding ring on the appropriate finger. Will believed that infidelity was the key to a happy marriage, but only fantasized infidelity—and only with other men. Denise had learned by observing her mother that homemaking and child rearing were to replace sex after marriage as the keys to marital fulfillment. However, Will was outraged at hearing about Karl's six month abstinence, thus beginning a therapeutic process in which the couples shared experiences over the weeks to come, as lack of satisfying sex became a focal theme for the entire group.

Because the group members genuinely enjoy and care about each other, a high level of interest in one another's problems soon develops and the discussion is quite animated. Although only one couple may be the focus of the group's attention at any time, most group members become involved in the discussion and contribute their observations and personal experiences related to the problem at hand. The therapists simultaneously focus attention on the couple in the foreground and on the group as a whole, thereby generating a wide range of intervention options (see Chapter 9) and a high level of involvement of all group members.

The biggest risk for the welfare of the group in this part of the session is getting bogged down in the particular issues of one couple and thereby losing the enthusiasm of the rest of the group. This problem, when it arises, usually emerges from one of two sources: The first is the monopolizing couple. This is frequently a couple with a rather entrenched marital problem which takes up a great deal of group time. At times, the same problem emerges in ever new forms without resolution of the underlying issue.

> Penny and Leo were one couple with a recurrent problem like this. For many sessions they came into the group session reporting on yet another marital battle. These battles appeared to be about novel problems, which they had not encountered before, and yet they had a repetitive quality to them. They also seemed to arise over trifles. One night, Penny and Leo came in with the report of a tremendous fight the previous week. Penny had been driving the car with Leo next to her. She pulled

up to a gas station and left too much space between the car and the gas pump, by Leo's standards. Leo roundly berated her for this, hurling insults and threats at her in the process. Penny fought back as best she could, letting him know she was sick and tired of being criticized for everything. After the screaming phase of the fight had been completed, there was cold-shouldered silence for the rest of the two-hour car ride.

Before this session other group members had already expressed displeasure with the repetitiveness of having to deal with Penny and Leo's fights in so many meetings. However, there also was compassion for this couple who were unable to stop these fights despite clear signs of love and devotion for each other. There appeared to be no resolution and the fights continued until one of the group members and one of the leaders discovered that the fights, including the one at the gas pump, tended to occur mostly when the couple was basically in a romantic mood and the possibility of sex and intimacy was close at hand. This gave the couple pause and the group was able to deal with intimacy and the avoidance of intimacy as a larger group problem which affected several couples. The group members also were able to help Penny and Leo to deal with their fear of intimacy in more constructive ways.

A second instance in which a group gets bogged down and loses enthusiasm occurs when a particular couple is struggling with an issue, but not bringing it up in the group for some reason. The reason may be shyness, shame, or the presence of other couples who simply happen to be more vociferous in bringing up issues.

Karl and Randy were so terrified of sexuality that they neglected to discuss it in the group and their individual therapy. Instead, in the two months preceding their active working phase on sexuality, they became quieter and quieter in the group. Asked "how are things going?" they would reply "Oh, fine — great."

Although the group and the therapists knew something was "fishy", they were unable to cut through the collusion which bound the couple into the stance of maintaining stability at any price. When, in an outside session, the issue of sex was approached and the topic was then taken into the group, there was a sense of relief in the group as a whole.

One way to guard against this risk is for the couple to schedule individual, couple, or family sessions at least once every three to four weeks. Such out-of-group therapeutic contacts are part of the pre-group contract and are an integral aspect of the treatment package.

Second half: Structured exercises   A brief five-minute break midway through the evening gives everyone the opportunity to stretch, walk around, get something to drink, etc. Couples also like to take this opportunity to share more trivial news with each other (restaurant reviews, cooking recipes, news of outings, vacations, or promotions). More significant news bulletins are reserved for the group session. The break functions like an intermission in a two-act drama. Members are respectful of "the break" and of sitting down to work again as the "second act" begins.

The second half of the session is usually reserved for structured exercises. These exercises are designed to increase the group members' understanding of an issue which seems to be "in the air," i.e., of concern to many group members at a given time (Wienecke, 1984). We actually choose or design the exercise during the five-minute break, in response to a common theme or prevailing emotion in the group. Thus, the exercise may focus on anger, fear of intimacy, sadness, affection, death, addictions, or other topics. Chapter 4 is devoted to designing, choosing, and conducting useful exercises in the second half of the group session.

"Class Outing": The Intensive Workshop

As part of the complete 11-month group experience, each group has a workshop in the Spring. We take the group participants out of their usual environment and conduct the workshop in a resort location. The usual workshop is two and a half hours in length. For a minimal fee, the group can elect to have an additional two and a half hours to make it a full-day workshop. Most groups choose to make it a full day.

The group chooses the topic of the workshop and everyone looks forward to it. The following themes, so far, have been tried by various groups: Sex and Intimacy, Life Planning and Marriage, Change vs. Stability, The Expression of Anger, and Getting Your Needs Met in a Couple without Alienating the One You Love.

In the workshop itself, couples work on the theme in a variety of ways. The leaders design a number of structured exercises which will approach the topic from different aspects. Once again, no "canned" exercises are used. The spontaneity unfolds from the uniqueness of the workshop which is designed for each particular group.

The workshop enhances the work that the couples are doing in the group. Being away from their usual environment, couples frequently are more relaxed, more intimate, and therefore more communicative with each other. Having more time to spend on one particular topic allows the couple to work it through in more depth and come to resolutions which may be harder to find when there is less time available.

Furthermore, the variety of structured experiences usually allows couples to deepen the insights gained earlier in the group experience. The following is an example of a typical workshop day. Further details about the fantasy are offered in the Appendix, and in Chapter 7.

A SAMPLE COUPLES GROUP WORKSHOP

TITLE: **Those who do not study history are doomed to repeat it: Moving on from your family of origin**

TIME ALLOTTED: Five working hours plus breaks

MEMBERS: Four couples in a couples group, two co-leaders

LOCATION: Beach resort office suite

TIME PLAN:

3:30–4:00. Reinvent my life story, using written handout. Each person has 10 minutes to write a few words about the two most important intimate relationships in his/her life, why each relationship was chosen, how painful each relationship was, and how the two relationships differed from one another.

4:00–4:30. Each person chooses a partner of the opposite sex other than their marital partner. Dyads discuss the earlier exercise in light of the current marriage. How did past relationships influence the current relationship? What does the person wish he or she had learned in the family of origin which could have helped the person to be different in the current relationship?

4:45–5:00. Break

5:00–5:20. NOAH'S ARK FANTASY. Induce relaxation (see instructions in Chapter 7). Leader speaks with slow pace and clear but soft tonality: Imagine that you and your spouse are not human. Instead, you are animals and you are going into Noah's Ark. Think about yourself and your spouse and your marriage. Which animals would you like to be? Search through the many species of birds, reptiles, mammals and fish until you find an animal pair that you would enjoy being. Now imagine that Noah orders you onto the Ark. Do you want to go? Does your spouse look forward to going? What is the feeling state of your animals? What are the advantages and disadvantages in going into Noah's Ark together? Imagine that you have no choice, so you and your spouse go into the Ark. What is life like for you there? Imagine you and your spouse as an animal pair in the Ark. What do you do? How do you relate to each other? How does it feel? Take a few moments to image you and your spouse now as the animals in the Ark. Leader brings members out of the fantasy by counting backwards, as described in Chapter 7.

5:20–5:30. Each member writes down the fantasy experienced during the guided imagery.

5:30–6:00. Each member demonstrates his or her fantasy in pantomime, using other group members as the animals involved. Each member has 10 minutes to be the actor or actress. Members perform by couples — first one partner in a couple demonstrates, then the other in order to give everyone a chance to see similarities in conscious and semiconscious fantasies about the marriage, as well as the differences in wishes, needs, and desires for each partner. Brief discussion of the issues follows each pair, so that the exercise flows as follows: couple demonstrates individually, followed by group discussion. Each dyad gets 20 minutes in total. This process occurs four times, and is ended by the leaders summarizing the themes, the importance of fantasy and desire in setting expectations in a marriage, and the centrality of themes from family and origin in creating theses unconscious fantasies.

6:00–7:30. Dinner break.

7:30–8:30. Finish fantasy acting and discussion.

8:30–9:00. Each marital dyad goes to a quiet corner and discusses the workshop experiences in depth, focusing on four questions: How much are the partners in agreement about their wishes for the marriage? How far have they come as a couple in making the desired changes? What is the next step in changing the relationship in the desired direction? Which attributes do the chosen animals have which are reflected currently, or which you would like to be reflected, in your marriage?

9:00–9:30. Magic Wand Exercise (see Appendix). Connect magic wand exercise to the family of origin and to the current relationship.

9:30–10:00. Group discussion of whole workshop and summarizing wrap-up by co-leaders. Discussion of how to use the workshop material in ongoing therapy work.

Noah's Ark: Four Couples Fantasies

The following descriptions are of those animals produced by a couples group in response to the instructions above. Each partner had a chance to create a fantasy, often disregarding the instructions given. Acting out and discussing the fantasy according to the above guidelines produced a multilevel learning experience for the workshop members.

Ellis and Jaime.   Ellis thought of animals as reflecting his marriage the way it is now, despite the instructions. He imagined a family of lions. The parents have the cubs fed, and the father lion is isolated off to the side, while the mother lion busies herself with her cubs. Jaime wished her marriage to be like gazelles. She imagined two graceful, lithe gazelles leaping together, taking turns being in the lead, looking out for each other's welfare, a challenging and playful match for each other.

Amy and Paul.　　Paul thought of herons, birds native to the beach resort where the workshop was held. The herons were pretty, and were feeding and preening, flying North and South with the seasons of the year. Amy imagined two doves, feeling relaxed, perched in a cool breeze high in the Ark, with the other animals below them.

Jerry and Tess.　　Jerry imagined two zebras lying in their stalls with all needs cared for. He said that zebras are like horses, but are more captivating because of their appearance. His zebra pair is lying, sides touching occasionally, feeling safe, secure, and content. Tess thought of love birds, Mommy and Daddy love birds, passing out worms to the babies in the nest. They are all content because there are plenty of worms.

Jack and Deirdre.　　Jack imagined a pair of otters, which he said are inseparable and mates for life. Without their mate, Jack said the otters die quickly. His otters have no natural enemies, play with each other, never go hungry, and can go anywhere they want. Deirdre was confused, and thought of a pair of animals from different species, which represent the marriage as it is now. She pictured an overly affectionate male dog and a stand-offish female cat. The cat looks around and plays hard to get, but really wants the dog to come over and chase her.

The workshop presents a rich opportunity for clinical work on a number of levels simultaneously, within the framework of enough time and distance from the daily grind of life to enable the richness of fantasy and cognitive reality to come together to make possible considerable change in a short period of time.

MIDYEAR EVALUATION AND TERMINATION

During the month of February the couples group reaches the halfway mark of the contract. At this time, the group takes another look at the goals which the couples had set for themselves in their assessment forms in the early phase of the group. This helps couples to get a sense of how much closer they have come in reaching their goals and to find out which couples are having trouble. Most of the time this review phase turns out to be an encouraging move which infuses the group with new energies, a renewed sense of direction, and a sense that time is moving on. Work to be done had best be gotten on with.

As the month of July draws nearer, couples have to deal with the inevitability of the "death" of their group. It is usually necessary for the therapists to hammer away at this reality. Most group members do not like to be reminded of death. They would rather continue working on the "hot" issues and enjoy the intimacy and cohesiveness that has been achieved, unencumbered by thoughts of leaving each other. Nevertheless, a constructive coping with the group's ending helps members deal with other termination issues in their lives, and proves to be a valuable learning experience. As Lee once put it: "Every year Judy tells us that the group is about to end and every year we ignore it."

With the realization that the group is about to end, the leaders force the couples to review their progress in terms of the goals which they had set for themselves in the Fall. At this point, some couples choose to re-contract for another year, while others will come to a completion of their group participation. Decisions regarding whether a couple are better off with another group year or not are made cooperatively by the couple in question, by the leaders, and by the other group members. Everybody gives feedback, advice, and suggestions, and differences in opinions are worked through. In this manner, the couple receive extremely valuable feedback on the progress which others see.

For many couples there is tremendous pride in seeing how far they have come in the opinion of their peers. Couples revisit the annoying habits and vicious cycles which brought them into the group in the first place and derive a sense of mastery from the successful resolution of past troublesome problems. The credit is rightfully theirs. They did the work. Frequently, the original conflict is still there in one form or another but solutions have been worked out which both partners can live with. These couples, in our opinion, are ready to "graduate," an expression which is quite commonly used amongst the group participants.

Other couples may decide that, despite the progress that has been made, they still need to learn more and change more. This does not mean that they feel bad because they do not "graduate": Usually they are encouraged by the progress they have made and it is precisely because of this encouragement that they want to deepen their learning through another year. Even though these couples will begin another round a little while later, their group as they know it terminates in July. Thus, they have to say farewell just as much as the others.

The final session is frequently a celebration of life, of love, and of partnership. Couples celebrate the "graduates" and say farewell to one another in a way which often turns out to be humorous, poignant, and very meaningful. Couples sometimes bring in food and sparkling cider to truly celebrate the progress made over the year. We frequently design a final structured exercise to enable people to say good-bye in an authentic way. An exercise like the following one gives everyone an opportunity to participate in one last round of giving feedback to each other, to the leaders, and to the group as a whole.

The Group Gift

At the end of one couples group, we gave everyone pencil and paper and 10 minutes to write their response to the following: "Imagine that it was within your power to give a gift to this group. Your gift can be anything — it can be a real object or it can be something abstract, like a fantasy; it can be for yourself, your partner, any other member, either or both leaders, or the group as a whole. As you reflect on your 11 months with us, what treasure would you like to give to this group?"

The answers were quite thought-provoking:

> *I have a symbolic gift for you. I want to give you your own personal luggage rack, because you carry a lot of baggage.*
> — *Ben to Ted*

> *I wish I could give you the gift of abandonment with being close to each other.*
> — *Lena to Karl and Randy*

CO-LEADERSHIP: MARRIAGE BETWEEN EQUALS

At this point, our couples groups are co-led by the authors. The male-female co-leadership of the group contributes to its efficiency. Co-leadership provides both a technical advantage and a therapeutic gain. Because there are two leaders, it is possible for the group to continue working even if one of the leaders has to be absent for professional or health reasons, vacations, out-of-town meetings, etc.

On a therapeutic level, the leaders provide a valuable complement to each other: If one of them either overlooks or exaggerates the importance of a particular issue at hand, the other one can provide a balance, bring in an additional point of view, and prevent potential iatrogenic problems. In solo-led groups, the group itself must provide this corrective, but it is valuable to have a leader provide this function for the group. Rutan and Stone (1984) list a variety of advantages of co-leadership but also point out its drawbacks, citing a number of authors who point out that the complexities of the relationship between the co-leaders may detract from the power of the group. Nevertheless, co-therapy is quite common as a leadership modality and the advantages outweigh the drawbacks for many group therapists.

It is a further advantage to the group if the leaders are of different genders (Kluge, 1974). Members of heterosexual couples have the opportunity to project their own feelings towards the opposite sex onto one of the leaders and work them out in the transference (Cividini & Klain, 1973; Cooper, 1976).

> In one of the groups, Jane, a lonely, bitter woman who was an office manager, had gotten an MA in Counseling Psychology years before. For a number of reasons, primarily lack of confidence in her skill and judgment, she never established herself as a mental health professional. Meanwhile, she had an affair with a much younger man. She chose not to tell her husband about this affair, a decision which began to weigh heavily on her around the time she entered treatment.
>
> In earlier groups, we as therapists were less clear about our position on such issues, and chose (mistakenly) not to push her to reveal her secret. Instead, she developed a distrust of Judith's ethicalness as a therapist, accusing her of "sloppy" handling of confidentiality, which no other group member agreed with. Jane began to discount Judith's handling of the group, saying that Erich was the therapist with the expertise. This projected distrust acted as a smokescreen, protecting Jane from her distrust in both her own judgment, and her ethicality as a woman.

In working with one another, it is essential that the co-leaders have a positive working relationship. They may have different therapeutic styles, but they still have to agree on their basic therapeutic theoretical frame. Considerable differences in the theory of what is helpful to people in a group could severely undermine the efficacy of the therapy (Hellwig & Memmott, 1974).

The therapists have to give each other room to unfold and to develop their best therapeutic abilities without fear of criticism by the other or of being undermined during the session. It must be possible for them to respectfully disagree with each other as differences occur, but there has to be an underlying belief in and even admiration for the other one's ability and competencies. Thus, when differences of opinion arise during the course of the group, group members have an opportunity to observe a successful conflict resolution and perhaps even learn from the modeling that is being presented by the leaders.

Whatever the relationship of the two therapists is outside of the group (colleagues, supervisor-supervisee, marriage partners, or good friends), it is crucial that that relationship be kept viable throughout the duration of the group. Difficulties are likely to arise, as they do in most human relationships, at some time or another, but an inability to resolve such difficulties within a reasonable amount of time is destructive to the group. Groups have a great interest in the relationship of the therapists to each other and some form of group fantasy usually exists as to the nature of their relationship. Signs of co-leader disharmony will be viewed by group members with great concern, especially since in most couples groups several members are products of disturbed marriages. In addition, there will be group members who—perhaps out of a need to recreate their family of origin in the group—will actually endeavor to sow disharmony between the leading couple (see Rutan & Stone, 1984).

Steve developed distrust towards one of us, as did Jane. But Steve developed distrust of Erich's masculinity, competence, and capacity for success. Steve was the son of a pharmacist in a small town who became depressed when Steve was born, and has remained depressed ever since, despite psychotherapy and medication. Part of Steve's decision to become a psychiatrist, was, in his opinion, an attempt to "turn his father into a real man," by lifting the depression. As a "fatherless" son, Steve came to both resent and be dependent on his mother's power within the family.

In the couples group, Steve would talk with the group about how he feared that we, as a therapy team, were not a team at all. He suspected that Erich was but an empty shell, and he re-coined an old phrase, "Behind every unsuccessful man there is an unhappy woman." The group worked with Steve, saying that while they certainly saw a difference in leadership styles, they also saw mutual respect and competence from each member of the therapy team.

It is also very important that the therapists have a common therapeutic posture regarding their own degree of self-disclosure. Any discrepancy in the levels of self-disclosure that emerges between the two therapists will give rise to some rather uncomfortable group dynamics: The group will come to see the more self-disclosing therapist as more open, loving, and accessible, but also probably as the weaker one, as some of the research on therapist self-disclosure has shown (see Coché & Dies, 1981, for a discussion of this issue). In order to prevent such typecasting, it is wiser for the therapists to have a common position on the level of the therapist self-disclosure which is acceptable to them.

The situation in which the two co-leaders are married to one other is a variant of other co-leadership situations (Low & Low, 1975). Everything that has been said above about the need for respect and admiration for the other's special therapeutic talents is particularly applicable to the co-leader team married to each other. Self-disclosure becomes an even more poignant issue with this type of co-leader team in that the group will naturally want to know as much as possible about how this couple has solved certain marital issues when they came up in their marriage. There is likely to be an even stronger push from the group to get the leaders to open up about themselves than there is already in any therapy group.

Some married-to-each-other group leaders may feel comfortable with using themselves as a model, whereas others might say that it is too much of an intrusion of the group into the marital dynamic. Some degree of intrusion is unavoidable. The group, after all, does give rise to all types of marital issues which the leading couple may or may not have resolved successfully for itself.

The rule of thumb regarding self-disclosure which we have adopted for ourselves is that the group receives no more self-disclosure than what it can observe in our actual within-group behavior. In the group session, the group is about to see how we interact with each other in a professional context and can see the manner in which we talk to each other, agree and disagree, and joke around with each other. Beyond this, however, we believe that more self-disclosure would only create dependency on us, which induces looking to the leading couple for "all the answers" rather than using one another as the resources for possible solutions to marital problems.

OUT-OF-GROUP PSYCHOTHERAPY WORK

Working with a therapist in individual, couple, or family sessions at least once every three weeks is a necessary part of the treatment package. Some group therapy practitioners disagree with this guideline and believe that such a procedure drains away energies from the group. In our experience, the other danger, that a couple's problem "falls through the cracks," is the larger concern.

There is some flexibility regarding who provides the out-of-group sessions. It is often one of the group therapists, but it can also be an outside therapist. If one of the group leaders also sees a couple outside of the group, this couple is likely to believe that it has a special relationship to this therapist and may feel superior to the other couples. It is important for the group leader to be aware of such transference issues and deal with them as needed (Ormont, 1981).

Furthermore, there have to be clearly spelled out rules between the therapist and the clients regarding the use of group material in individual sessions and the use of individual session material in the group. We ask that all agree that anyone — client or therapist — can bring material into the group if appropriate. We assume that everyone will use good judgment as to what kind of material to leave out of the group. Furthermore, we agree with Pittman (1989) that affairs need to be discussed within marital treatment, regardless of whether this treatment is in a group or a couples sessions.

Marci had an affair. She refused to raise it in the group, or to tell her husband. Despite clear concerns expressed by family and friends about her judgment, Marci held steadfastly to her decision not to talk about this except in individual sessions with her individual therapist. After months of readiness building, Marci finally came to understand that the secrecy was worse than the crime and that secrecy was the more serious marital disrupter.

A different set of issues arises when a couple is seen by an outside therapist. A particular transference issue which can arise in this case is "splitting" — picturing one person as all good and another as all bad (Cooper, 1976; Wells, 1985). In a maneuver not unfamiliar to most therapists, a couple (or an individual) may come to see one therapist (e.g., the group leader) as the "good parent" and the other as the "bad" one. The group leaders must avoid getting hooked into this by becoming defensive or by agreeing to criticisms of the outside therapist. The problem can then be dealt with therapeutically and benefit the couple considerably.

Splitting also occurs within the group by the setting off of one leader as good and the other as bad, but this is more obvious and easier to deal with as long as the leaders are a unified team which has its own issues of competition well in control. If they do not, however, they can easily fall into the trap, consciously or unconsciously support the splitting, and battle with it. The situation is quite analogous to children playing off one parent against the other and interpretations of this nature are appropriate and helpful.

Finally, working with an outside therapist requires coordination and integration. It is of utmost importance that the outside therapist and the group leaders maintain communication. They have to inform each other of important events in each setting and agree on the major therapeutic goals and the main pathways to achieve them. Here, too, it is crucial that they support and respect each other in their work.

WHAT MAKES COUPLES GROUP PSYCHOTHERAPY EFFECTIVE?

The treatment package presented here has a variety of ingredients which contribute to a constructive psychotherapy experience. Many of the ingredients could be varied to fit the needs of a different setting. However, even if it varies, it is the complete package which helps the couples to work through their issues in the most useful manner.

The two most important ingredients are the couples work and the group work. The presence of the partner allows the other people in the group to see the couple in action and to give firsthand observations on the way in which the partners "wind each other up" to have an argument, set traps for each other, and avoid intimacy.

In addition, all the curative factors of a group come into play. Ever since Yalom's (1975) first efforts to formalize the ways in which groups are therapeutic, more and more has been understood about these ways and how they occur at different stages of the group. We find that in the early stages of the therapy group, *universality* plays an important role in getting couples going, while in the middle phases *learning from each other* appears to be the crucial ingredient. Furthermore, due to its particular composition of members, each group develops its own style of working. Thus, while *insight* may be crucial in some groups, *experiential learning, altruism,* and *receiving feedback* may be much more important in others.

Moreover, the group represents a microcosm of a marital community in which couples show their interactive style. The necessity for individuals in the couple to relate to a variety of people creates opportunities to see more clearly—for example, whether a husband in the group shows condescending behavior only towards his spouse, or with all women, or with all people.

3.

Establishing and Maintaining Workable Group Policies

The harder course is not to reduce one's life to rigid formulas,
but to recognize and live with life's ambiguities.

—André

THE WISDOM OF HAVING GROUP POLICIES

Consistent and clearly spelled out group policies are part of intelligent group psychotherapy preparation. The literature (Mayerson, 1984; Coché & Coché, 1986; Nichols, 1976) demonstrates that well-prepared group participants have a better concept of what they are supposed to do. They also have a higher expectation that their group will be successful. Well-prepared groups, as was discussed in Chapter 1, build cohesiveness more speedily and have lower rates of absences and dropouts. One of the most significant aspects of group preparation is clarity about the group rules.

Group policies provide an outer frame within which the group process can unfold and flourish. If all participants, leaders, and members have the same conceptual framework in respect to the boundaries within which everyone operates, an atmosphere of safety develops. Inside these boundaries the group can pursue its task of improving marriages rather than using group time for interminable debates over group rules.

Some group theorists believe that such group debates aimed at creating the group's own work rules are cohesion-building and therapeutic. Such debates can aid in setting the expectation that the group is responsible for its own processes and should not depend on the leaders to tell the members what to do. While that is a valuable procedure in groups of professionals organized for the purpose of studying their own group process (as in Sensitivity Training or Group Process Education groups), we believe that such a procedure is inefficient for therapy groups. In therapy, clients are not focused on the intricacies of group processes. Instead, they are coming for help with their personal or marital problems and are relying on the leaders to create a group structure in which successful therapy can take place. Giving every participant a clear idea of what is expected helps the group to get underway without undue delay. It does not eliminate the need for discussions of the rules, but prevents the rules from being too much in focus.

The policies for the couples groups are a modification of policies which operate for all psychotherapy groups in the authors' practice. General policies were developed by the first author over the last decade of clinical work. They are in keeping with group norms advocated by other authors and clinicians in the group psychotherapy field (Rutan & Stone, 1984; Hoffman, personal communication.) These procedures work especially well in moving a group quickly to a cohesive working state. For the most part, the policies are just as useful for intensive group psychotherapy for adult individuals; specific to *couples* groups is only the policy which deals with partner absences.

The policies proposed here are derived from three sources: Clinical experience, the group psychotherapy literature, and client feedback. Many of the rules we use in the conduct of the couples groups have been debated at some length in the literature on group psychotherapy. In instances where there was no agreement on the best course of action, we were able to rely on our own clinical experience and that of our mentors and colleagues. The following vignette presents an instance of learning from experience:

A number of years ago our groups had no specific rules regarding out-of-session contacts or "socializing." The literature in this regard was quite contradictory at that time. While some authors were advocating that the group meet without their leaders on some occasions, maybe even regularly in so-called "alternate sessions," (Kutash & Wolf, 1983) other authors warned that this could create certain group dynamics over which the leader had very little or no influence and which could be harmful to the group (Wolf, 1983).

At that time, a woman in one of our non-couple groups was having a party at her house to which she invited some but not all group members. The leader was not informed that group members had been invited. There was an expressed expectation that the invited guests would not tell the rest of the group. This alone already set up a very uncomfortable situation, with part of the group containing a secret from the rest.

Even worse, some group members got into a fight at the party, which they then could not discuss in the group. Then word leaked out anyway. The feelings of rejection, isolation, guilt, and rage engendered by the event and its aftermath greatly reduced the therapeutic efficacy of that group. The incident taught us that out-of-group contacts can be very destructive to group work and that groups work better if the members know from the start what the limits of acceptable contacts between members are.

Many of the rules may appear self-evident. One might even ask why we would bother to spell them out. The answer is that many of these rules were formulated after we learned from experience that a given rule was not self-evident to everybody who joined our groups. That is understandable when one considers how anxious and vulnerable members of a new therapy group are.

THE CONTENT OF THE GROUP POLICIES

The following section presents the group policies as they are spelled out to prospective group members. While some of these rules are the same for all groups, others are specific to couples groups. Many are responses to important ethical concerns, while others are more mundane technical matters.

Out-of-Group Contacts

As the example above shows, interactions among group members between sessions can under certain circumstances be quite destructive. As long as a group is in existence, it is in the members' best interest if their contact outside of the group be kept to a minimum. Naturally, people will walk from the office to the parking garage together or they may have a chat on the sidewalk before going home from a group session. We strongly advise, however, that they keep their conversation light and not discuss group matters, especially not matters concerning other group members. Should some significant discussions arise anyway, their content is to be brought back to the group. As our group rule sheet shows, invitations to one another's houses are not permitted as long as both parties involved are still participating in the group. There is still quite a debate in the literature about the advisability of the "no socializing" rule (Flapan & Fenchel, 1983; Rutan, Alonso & Molin, 1984).

Commitment to a Closed-Group Experience

All of our couples groups are closed-ended; this means that all couples begin their group year together in September and stay together until the following July at which time a couple may "graduate," sign up for another 11-month period, or choose to pursue other treatment options.

In order for the model to work, couples have to make a firm commitment to stay in the group for the full 11-month duration. While on rare occasions it may be unavoidable that a couple must leave (e.g. because a partner is being transferred to another city and the family is relocating), a dropping out for any less pressing reason constitutes a serious breach of the contract and would cause considerable harm to the integrity of the group. All couples understand this mutual dependence on each other and are, therefore, loyal to their group and consistent in their attendance. Once couples are convinced of the considerable psychological and therapeutic benefits of closed membership they are usually willing to make the time commitment and stick to it.

Dealing With Partner Absences

Occasionally it is unavoidable for a group member to miss a session. At these times, we expect the partner of the absent member to attend. We have found that the sessions in which only one member of a couple is present are often very fruitful for the attending partner, especially if that partner was stifled in his or her participation by the spouse.

Catherine originally joined the group only for Todd. Todd was superbright, super-ambitious, super-successful, and felt super-empty inside half of any calender year. Todd, the son of an alcoholic father, had learned by age seven to trust himself over anyone else, regardless of age or position. His first marriage ended in failure, as did Catherine's. The second time around both were determined not to make a mistake, and both partners believed that Todd knew better on most issues, even though Catherine left a management position in retailing to marry her Superhero, and was considered by the group to be attractive, well-dressed, intelligent, socially adept, and, perhaps, just a touch too perfect for anyone to get too close to.

For months, Catherine maintained that she had no problems other than Todd's problems and that, in fact, she would be happy if someone in the group could find a problem for her so she would feel her time in the group was being better invested. When members pointed out that denial might be something she'd want to consider, she denied that denial was an issue for her. And so the group progressed.

One evening, when Todd was in Europe on business, Catherine, good at following instructions, came alone to the group although she was not sure why. We asked her how it felt to be in the group as a solo individual and she stated that it felt strange. Yet when asked how it felt to be without Todd, she allowed that it felt sort of normal, since he was psychologically absent much of the time even when he was physically present. But she assured us that she wasn't angry. After all, how could she be angry at such a nice, hardworking man?

A woman in the group said she would be angry if she were Catherine, since Todd's mood shifts and withdrawal controlled Catherine's life.

Little by little for the next 30 minutes, Catherine began to feel angry at Todd for the first time. She was reminded of her first husband, who had psychologically abandoned her before physically leaving. She was angry at her family, who were so polite and socially graceful that she hardly knew them. And she was angry with Todd in a way she never would or could have allowed had he been present and angry at the way in which his psychological withdrawal dominated her and the group.

Dealing With Confidentiality

Confidentiality is the most important policy in any therapy. A group cannot function unless members trust that their personal self-disclosures are held in confidence by the other members (Davis & Meara, 1982). Group participants are told that they are not to divulge the names or information about the lives of other group members to anyone. They may talk about their own struggles and changes in therapy with others but not about the changes in other group members' lives.

New group participants are informed about this rule before they join the group and again during the first session. Within the first 30 minutes of a new group, they sign a confidentiality agreement and discuss the rule as it is written in the sheet of policies. In so doing it becomes very clear that confidentiality is the cornerstone of good group therapy.

Dealing With Financial Obligation

Members pay the monthly fee for all sessions of a month at the time of the first group session of that month. They receive a statement of their account at the beginning of the next month for insurance and record-keeping purposes. Sessions are to be paid for regardless of absence. It is the complete group experience which is therapeutic; therefore, people also pay for a session which they might have to miss. Members are aware of this rule at the time they agree to join the group.

If a couple have not paid for the month by the second session of the month, the therapist who functions as the "keeper of the structure" reminds them in the group. If a couple falls behind in payment, it is a therapeutic issue to be dealt with in their couples session or in the group. If there is a genuine hardship situation, special arrangements can be made. However, couples are told to ask for special arrangements *before* they fall behind, not later.

Concurrent Adjunctive Psychotherapy Work

In order for the group to be maximally effective, couples need individual, couples, or family sessions between their group sessions. Most couples feel the need for additional therapeutic work aside from the group and schedule their sessions accordingly. Occasionally, however, a couple resists the therapy and delays scheduling meetings between group sessions. By the time the resistance becomes obvious to the group, it is already quite late and important therapeutic momentum may have been lost. Clinical experience has shown us that the couples who got least from the group were often those who "slipped through the cracks" and did not schedule their own couples sessions. When this was finally discovered, the group had moved on developmentally and the couple did not gain as much from the experience as it could have.

Working with couples in a group is actually a process of working with individual adults in intimate partnership with other individual adults in the company of other individual adults who are in intimate partnership with one another. Explained in this manner, the rationale for additional psychotherapy sessions becomes clear to those in the group.

Change is maximized by enabling members to reflect on their in-group experience both inside and outside of the group itself. A couple may choose to discuss its individual or couples session in the group, and often does. Usually, when an individual or couple want to use a session outside of the group to discuss group business, the therapist listens to the issue and encourages the persons to raise the issue in the next group meeting.

Judith often tells clients that the group is "like popcorn popping," and that there is so much going on in a short period of time that work outside of the group enables the members to process the learning and to individualize it to their lives as individuals and as part of a couple. The treatment package is thus conceptualized as a combination of modalities which is tailor-made to suit the needs of each couple at each stage of their psychotherapy.

Serge and Suzanne are the ultimate two-career young family, with two adorable toddlers and more extra-career activities than most couples without children could handle. There is the church work and the gourmet cooking group and the professional societies and the celebrations of elaborate dining with friends and the graduate work and, of course, visits to each partner's family at holidays. Into this camp-like schedule Serge and Suzanne, who are quite well organized, managed to fit in the time for the couples group and, in the first year of the group, for adjunctive sessions as well.

They progressed slowly as the group helped them to come to terms with the function of their hectic style of living in assuring that they spent little intimate time together. What we neglected to notice was that the couple, and Serge in particular, were drifting away from the adjunctive therapy work just as he got closer and closer to the issues (lack of intimacy, experienced quite painfully) which brought them to therapy in the first place. Time moved on, and Serge and Suzanne grew more and more helpful to other members in the group, and no one noticed that they were in pain, least of all they, themselves.

Months later, Serge came to us and said that he was really angry at us for not confronting him on his withdrawal, and that he planned to handle his anger by withdrawal . . . to a different individual therapist for himself. This time he intended to find someone who would not let him get away with his tricks, as Suzanne, his first wife, and his mother had done. Despite our invitation to stay and get closer to us by fighting the battle out, he seemed intent on withdrawing, saying that we "had missed our chance," just as his father and mother had done in his opinion.

PROCEDURES TO IMPART GROUP POLICIES

Group rules are so important that it is advisable to communicate them to new clients several times and in different ways. The screening interview, which usually is a couples therapy session in which the suggestion that this couple join the group is discussed, is the first time the procedures are mentioned. Secondly, couples receive a written copy of the group therapy policies. The confidentiality rule is so important that it is written up separately as a contract which everybody signs in the first group session (i.e. in everyone's presence). Thirdly, the first group session starts with a review of the policies while all couples are present. Questions are answered. Disagreements are discussed. The policies go into effect by the middle of the first meeting.

In the following example, the group rules are explained to new members:*

JC: Welcome to the couples group. We ask that you respect the policies and procedures of the group. We ask that you maintain the strictest confidentiality about your names and your lives outside of this room. We ask that you not socialize with one another for the duration of your membership in this group.

Will: Does that mean we can't get together for a drink afterwards?

JC: Yes, it does Will. We ask that all of the energy remain in the group. We also expect that you will work with your own therapist outside of the group, on the average of once every three weeks. That way, the learnings in the group will be intensified.

Nate: One concern I have is that I'm going to be out of town at times. I would imagine that I would miss five sessions of this group.

---

*Transcript from the videotape, *Techniques in Couples Group Therapy.*

JC: Well, Nate, we have built absences into the group. We expect that people will be absent because of illness, an emergency, or some sort of family business or travel. We ask that you tell the group before you will be absent because the group misses its absent members.

Lee: Judy, does that mean that if Nate's not here I should come anyway?

JC: Yes, absolutely, Lee. The group is actually a group for individuals who are in partnership with one another. You will benefit each time you come. We ask that you be forthright and honest as much as you possibly can in this group. That's the way you will get the most from it. And although that's a little bit frightening at first, the best way to overcome the fear is to simply take the plunge.

Discussing the Group Policies Before the First Session

Group psychotherapy preparation starts in the screening session in which the idea of joining a therapy group is first broached. In order to convey a sense of safety to the prospective group member, a couple is informed about issues like confidentiality and the commitment for the group's duration. In this discussion, it is very important to convey these policies not as dictates from above, but instead as parts of a larger framework which has been developed over years and has been found to be advantageous to people in groups. The goal is to obtain agreement from the participants and cooperation in functioning within these boundaries, not only because they respect the therapist who relays these guidelines, but because the new members also believe that these regulations are in the couple's best interest and are the building blocks of a group treatment approach which has been designed to maximize therapeutic efficacy.

The Written Statements of Policies

In mid-August, group members begin gearing up for the next round which begins in September. At that time, each couple receives a packet from us by mail. In addition to a welcoming letter, the packet contains the written statement of the policies and a schedule of all meetings and workshops scheduled for the next year of the group.

Two weeks before the group begins, members receive a call from our office manager, telling them the names of the other group members, and making sure that there is no conflict of interests we may have missed arising from members who have outside contacts being in the same group. For example, one year we caught a supervisor and supervisee about to be in the same group.

By the first meeting, each member has had ample opportunity to read the policies and procedures, which have been mailed to the new group members before the first group session. These sheets are updated annually as new, unforeseen problems arise and policies are created to prevent a recurrence of those problems. The couples are asked to read the policies before the first meeting. Then they have the opportunity to discuss the rules in the group and in their respective couples therapy sessions.

Recapitulation in First Session

The first session begins with a recapitulation of the policies. A good deal of time is spent on this quite purposefully. One of the therapists reviews the rules (as set down on the Policies sheet) one by one. The tone is declarative and low key. It neither sounds like a reading of the Ten Commandments, nor is it meant to be a selling job. It would be a mistake and would set the wrong tone for the group if the leader were long-winded and/or authoritarian in this presentation. If that were to happen, the group would be in danger of becoming much too dependent on a leader who is perceived as extremely powerful; it would set people up either for passivity (and therefore boring group meetings) or for a rather dramatic—though not necessarily therapeutic—phase of counterdependence a few sessions later (Bion, 1960).

Instead, the task of rule presentation is one of explanation, aimed at fostering discussion and ultimately at obtaining agreement based on understanding. As in the prior (individualized) discussion, we want the whole group to understand the wisdom of these guidelines and want the members to agree because they are convinced that these rules are designed to enhance their treatment.

Furthermore, while the rules are being reviewed, members understand this as an invitation to discuss what is being presented. In this process, it also becomes clear that although most of the policies will not be changed simply because a group member prefers it, policies are certainly discussible. People understand that the leaders are interested in the feelings engendered by certain rules and respect these reactions though there are some definite limits to the power a group has in trying to "overrule" the leaders.

It is very important to avoid misunderstandings in this regard early on. A group which later finds that it has a good deal less power than it was originally led to believe will become quite frustrated. The frustration can lead to either a resigned passivity or a very angry counterdependence. Therefore, the leaders need to be clear as to the limits of flexibility inherent in the group's policies.

One of the opportunities offered to the group is to be taped by a post-graduate intern in the Fall. In this way, members can view their own group at their convenience. In order for the taping to occur, the group needs to agree that they want it done. Occasionally, a member, especially a member who is either suspicious or extremely self-conscious, absolutely does not want the taping done. Yet at times this member may feel shy about being assertive enough to take the veto power.

> One year, Alysse, a very overweight woman who was terrified of being confronted with her appearance, disagreed with many of the policies and procedures and kept the group involved in a lengthy procedural discussion as a way to prevent the group from deciding whether to tape or not to tape. After a thorough discussion of the disagreements regarding policy, the issue of Alysse's feelings of powerlessness in the group were addressed directly and the group honored her terror by agreeing not to tape the group that Fall. Had this discussion not occurred, Alysse might have been frozen in her capacity to participate in and benefit from the group which she had so looked forward to joining.

THE KEEPER OF THE STRUCTURE

When working in a co-leader team, we have found it advantageous to have one of the leaders designated as the "keeper of the structure." This person is the one who pays particular attention to the boundaries of the group. He/she sees to it that the group starts and ends on time, that people pay their fees when they are supposed to, and that other structural policies are kept as agreed.

This kind of task assignment between the leaders is not meant as a rigid role division, but instead as a difference in cognitive emphasis and attention. It also helps to avoid "slip-ups," as when people break group rules like paying on time and nobody notices. Most of the time, the group itself will see to it that its rules are being maintained. People who arrive late more than once are usually told by other group members how disruptive it is. Having a keeper of the structure, however, provides the safeguard that someone will enforce group rules when the group does not do so on its own.

The "keeper of the structure" is useful for both training purposes and general clinical effectiveness. It was developed by the first author as part of the training program in group psychotherapy in the author's practice. When used in a senior-junior co-therapy team, as is the case in a training program, the junior leader naturally functions as the keeper of the structure. Time, absences, money, furniture, these are the physical symbols of the relationship between group members and leaders. In a senior therapist combination, as occurs when we co-lead the couples groups, we still recommend that one co-leader be the keeper of the structure, but that the roles be richly interwoven beyond this job. In this way, the structural elements are handled without much fuss, but things are also not allowed to slip by because neither leader has felt fully responsible. In this way, the group is free to function without undue energy expenditure on mundane matters.

PART II

Psychotherapy with Couples in Groups

4.
Treatment Skills with Intimate Partners

I really think that our relationship is a great love story . . . the
great love story.

— Roy, married 25 years

A group in which couples are the members is only as effective as the clinical work being done with each couple in and outside of the group. The clinical work we do with couples precedes their entering the group and most often lasts beyond the last group meeting, as couples leave the group to try their newly-won skills and marital changes without the continued support of a group behind them. In this chapter, we review key concepts in the work with the couples in their therapies, in group, and otherwise.

Couples work is a vast clinical body of thinking, practice, and research. Much of the work which applies to couples is actually found in the literature in family therapy (Whitaker & Keith, 1981; Whitaker & Bumberry, 1988; Satir, 1967; Keeney & Silverstein, 1986) since much of the pioneering family work was not specifically created for the unit of intimate partners without their children. Other work has been specifically addressed to clinicians interested in the marital unit (Gurman, 1985; Bader & Pearson, 1988). Still other work comes out of the field of individual psychotherapy, but can be integrated, with some variation, into ongoing work with couples (Bugental, 1981, 1984; Rogers, 1957; Wexler & Rice, 1974; Truax & Carkhuff, 1967).

Our discussion will be highly pragmatic in nature, since our experience in training indicates that clinicians need hands-on knowledge of clinical techniques. However, we shall refer the reader to original sources. Our own methods have derived from personal and professional growth experiences with Whitaker, Silverstein, and Bugental, and from reading and teaching existential psychotherapy, family, and group therapy. These opportunities, some cognitive and academic, others highly experiential, provided us with a foundation within which to frame the experiences we have had with the couples groups, and the years of experience in clinical work which each of us has had. Without the supervised training experiences and original readings to fall back on, many of the most confusing clinical situations with these couples, both in the group and out of it, might have badly shaken our confidence in our work and in the still-developing fields of clinical psychology and group and family therapy.

In this chapter, we will also provide the philosophical foundations underlying the couples work and, to some extent, the group work we do. The most practical interventions with couples, as well as with clients in general, can sometimes be to give them a philosophical frame within which to structure their lives. This is a way in which we pass on the tools, the building blocks of a world view which is quite different from the world view in the families of the clients who come to us for help. In this chapter, we discuss our rationale for the therapeutic choices we have made for the couples we work with.

INDUCING CIRCULAR THINKING

We begin with a short discussion of the principles of circular thinking and isomorphism in couples theory and then discuss the existential foundations of our work. After presenting some key concepts, we shall describe the intergenerational focus in the couples therapy. We discuss our existential and strategic-based view of the dialectic of human change, and conclude by explaining briefly why and how we actually teach couples to think as systemically as family therapists. By the time someone graduates from a couples group, he or she often thinks more systemically about his own life than some clinicians we have met who are trained in a model of psychotherapy which is individual in nature. In this chapter, we show how this process occurs.

Inducing circularity of thinking is one of the simplest, but most useful, skills in a couples' therapist's repertoire (Selvini-Palazzoli et al., 1980). It can be taught to a couple, a family, or a beginning family therapist. Judith learned it from Olga Silverstein after a decade of doing family work, and has been using it daily ever since. It is useful to think of causality in human experience as circular, not linear.

What is meant by this is the following: Instead of the usual thinking underlying most scientific thought and much of behavioral psychology, that A causes B which causes C, and so on, it is useful to think in terms of a reactive process which involves A, B, and C. A impacts on B which is also influenced by C; B adjusts to A in a way which modifies (strengthens or lessens) the signals given out by A. B's "response" is the result of a series of quick and often minute exchanges between the participants in which each affects the other and is in turn affected by him/her/it. The causality for the event which then occurs is interpersonal, systemic, and dependent on the views which A, B, and C have in relation to each other and to the reactive pattern among them.

Applying this paradigm to our work with couples, it means that we also teach them that all reality in psychotherapy is *relative* (not absolute) to the parties who view it and *interpersonal* in nature, being dependent on the persons involved. Therefore, it follows that a view of reality which is relative and interpersonal can be shifted by the parties involved, and that any person in the system has the capacity to greatly affect the reality and, therefore, the behavior and thinking of anyone else in the system.

Moreover, we believe that couples need information about new ways to construct reality and that some couples are able to grasp the concepts presented above if presented in a concrete and interesting manner. Therefore, as early as the initial consultation, we begin to educate couples about how to ask new questions about old problems. We begin to show to them how the problem shifts from an impossible, earth-shattering dilemma to something more manageable once the view of the problem moves from being linear to being circular. Further, we believe that until members of a couple are able to move to this circular view of relationships, a couple is severely hampered in its capacity to solve marital dilemmas on their own.

Erik came to psychotherapy because he was worried about his wife's depression. He was not worried about his marriage, although the couple could not argue and threatened divorce when the going got too unpleasant. He was not worried about his pattern of intimacy, although this was a second marriage for both Erik and Nan. He was not worried about his relationship with his mother, although he admitted that if his wife refused to be less important in his life than his mother, he had no choice but to divorce Nan.

At his initial session, he behaved like a concerned family member who was seeing "the doctor" about his wife's illness. This behavior, much to his surprise, took a new twist when he and Nan actually met with Judith, "the doctor." Judith scheduled a battery of psychological tests for Nan, but (in Erik's eyes) seemed curiously disinterested in concentrating on her depression. Instead, she asked Erik how he reacted when Nan was down. If he tried to cheer her up but she became withdrawn, how did he feel and behave? How did he feel when Nan seemed particularly down at their weekly dinners at his mother's house?

Judith asked Nan which of the two family members, Erik or his mother, was least responsive to listening to how Nan felt at the dinner table. She asked Nan how each reacted if she mentioned that she would prefer to do something else occasionally. Then she asked Nan how Nan reacted to their response and whether any changes in the pattern of dinner and depression had been attempted.

Through this initial course of nonevaluative, interested questioning, the couple spoke about topics which had never occurred to them before. At the end of this first consultation, Nan had already begun to catch on to the importance of the interpersonal feedback loop in maintaining her clinical depression, although she was not yet strong enough to do much about it. Erik, on the other hand, kept asking, "Well, this is all very interesting, Judith, but what does it have to do with *Nan*? I mean, what are we to do about how depressed she is?" Much more work was obviously needed.

ISOMORPHISM IN TREATMENT MODALITIES

Elsewhere, the principle of isomorphism is discussed as it applies to work within the group. The principle, which states that processes which operate at one level of functioning are simultaneously operating at other levels as well, is a useful way to understand the rationale behind the combination of in-group and out-of-group treatment which we use and recommend. The couples work, which helps people to overcome obstacles to intimacy, improves the functioning of the couple. At the same time, it leads to benefits to each individual in the couple. As a result, the higher the functioning in the members, the greater the benefit to the group. Conversely, building cohesiveness skills in the group models intimate relationship behavior for the couple, and models effective interpersonal behavior for the individuals in the group.

Finally, working as a couple is a gift to their next generations. Again, by the principle of isomorphism, work done in one generation benefits other generations in a family. Thus, the integration of the couples work with group and individual work builds a psychotherapy momentum for the group and each of its members which is hard to duplicate when any single modality is utilized without the others.

AN EXISTENTIAL FOUNDATION FOR THE
PROCESS OF CHANGE

We offer clients an existential foundation within which to view the process of behavioral and interpersonal change. Through clinical interventions and our use of self, we teach and model a number of concepts basic to a way of being in the world, as well as to ways in which we believe people in couples and in families can experience constructive and lasting personal and interpersonal change.

Often, we rely on contributions from existential philosophy (Nietzsche, 1960; Sartre, 1948; Kaufmann, 1975) and from philosopher-theologians (Buber, 1958; Tillich, 1952) as conceptual underpinnings to the work at hand. Within the professional mental heath literature, we rely most heavily on the thinking of Whitaker et al. (1981, 1988, 1989), Bugental (1981, 1984), Watzlawick (1978, 1983, 1984), and Watzlawick, Weakland and Fisch (1974), although each has been modified to work within our fast-paced, somewhat more cognitive, highly systemic model.

We have, on many occasions, assigned sophisticated clients some readings to do at home: Napier & Whitaker's *The Family Crucible* (1978); Watzlawick's *The Situation is Hopeless but not Serious* (1983); Buber's *I and Thou* (1958); Fromm's *The Art of Loving* (1956); and Tillich's *The Courage to Be* (1952). Clients often report that the reading is worth the time and effort even though it is more demanding than the popular psychology they are used to finding on their own.

Existential psychotherapy is an extremely varied field with many very individualistic thinkers. Yet there are some common unifying principles. We will discuss here three of the conceptual underpinnings especially important in our work with couples:

1. Clients seek to be more of a person in an intimate context.
2. Adult intimacy involves taking responsibility for the self.
3. Clients need to exercise life choices.

1. Clients Seek to Be More of a Person in an Intimate Context

We agree with Whitaker and Keith (1981) that the goals of psychotherapy are to establish a sense of belonging, to provide the freedom for persons to individuate, and to increase personal and systemic creativity. Fundamentally, people enter psychotherapy to learn to be more of a person than they have been able to figure out from their life experience to date. Another way of saying this is that, although everyone seems to desire more intimacy than they have been able to achieve, the obstacles they construct maintain stability within the personality structure. Being more of a person means to free up new levels of energy and creativity by overcoming some of the obstacles which have been constructed by oneself and by one's family. This, in turn, creates a sense of greater personal freedom without necessitating the same unsuccessful behaviors. Meaning is increased and the person or couple need no longer return to the earlier and frustrating modus operandi.

2. Adult Intimacy Involves Taking Responsibility for One's Actions

Intimacy is at its best for adults when each partner is able to take responsibility for his/her own thoughts, feelings, and behavior in relation to the other person. Therefore, adult intimacy is best achieved when partners are skillful and careful in their communication with one another. This translates into learning to respect personal boundaries in being close to someone else, regardless of one's background.

This way of viewing intimacy also translates into the necessity for each person to learn how he/she feels, to learn how to communicate feelings, to learn to listen to the thoughts and feelings of another person, and to negotiate conflict in a respectful manner. These are skills which we teach couples.

3. Living Life Fully and Responsibly Entails Making Life Choices

No matter what happens in life, each person is faced with continual choices. On a large scale, big life choices for the most part belong to the person, barring unforeseen natural disasters and illnesses beyond one's control. People have to decide, for the most part, whether and when to divorce or separate, when and whether to have and raise children, how to feed and care for their body and intellect.

We are not saying that people are to blame for the choices they make, but rather that it is part of living life fully that people own their choices as a way of enjoying their pleasures and learning from their own mistakes. Choices are often made on the basis of hidden existential conflicts which are echoed in the legacy inherited by children growing up in a family which was in a painful situation in the world. During childhood and adolescence, the powerful force of the family of origin with all its beliefs, traditions, and adaptive styles handed down through generations, exerts its pull and shapes the person's beliefs about the ways in which decisions are to be made. Because we have these assumptions, we often magnify the existential theme for a couple who seem to be struggling with a common, everyday problem. To their surprise, drawing attention to the larger existential issue often opens new ways to "unstick" the everyday dilemma.

Don and Danielle married despite family concerns over the fact that he was Jewish and she was Catholic; both had been warned not to marry outside their religion. Less than three months after the wedding, they became obsessed with "how to raise the children" although they did not plan to have children for at least three years. Which religion to raise the children in became a haunting argument, and Don finally sought treatment, not to receive help with the decision regarding the children, but because he became disablingly depressed.

As treatment progressed, Danielle was happy to also have some help with "how to raise the children" and we began to explore the meaning for each family of origin of marrying into the other faith. The couple actually went to members of each side of the family as part of a homework assignment and invited the families to discuss their views on the other religion.

What the couple learned was very enlightening: Danielle, raised Catholic, said that she had been told that Jews could not be trusted. Don learned that Christians had been, in his family's opinion, responsible for the deaths of many of Don's great aunts and uncles in the second World War, and were not to be trusted. The couple began to realize that they were caught in a battle not of their own making. This realization marked the beginning of new approaches to their dilemma.

At this time, a few years later, there are indeed children. Christmas and Chanukah are celebrated, and the couple enjoy sharing each other's traditions. Danielle decided to allow the formal education to be both liberal and Jewish because of the warmth she felt in relation to a congregation which Don belonged to. Relating the issue to larger existential themes enabled the couple to change their perspective and to take matters into their own hands. Then they were able to resolve the conflict.

The same principle operates on a smaller scale. Regardless of how ridiculous the behavior of a spouse may seem, the other partner has options in how to respond. Knowing this and learning skillful ways to exercise the options give both spouses a feeling of control over at least their part of a situation. For example, when Danielle would yell at Don that he was ill-behaved at her church, he could remind her gently that he didn't know how to behave in a Catholic church, but would be happy to learn if she could calm down and teach him. When he would scream that no Christmas tree was ever coming through his front door, Danielle could hold tight and wait for the opportunity to remind him that it was, in fact, *their* front door and they would have to negotiate it as a couple. Both partners have learned to make their individual choices within the context of interpersonal relationships which exist in the present, in the past of each family, and in the history of the world in which the families had developed.

AN INTERGENERATIONAL FRAME FOR COUPLES WORK

The last few paragraphs already point to the second conceptual frame for our work with couples which is intergenerational in nature. This conceptual frame has two important clinical consequences:

1. Those who understand family history are not doomed to repeat it.
2. Current couple conflicts always relate to issues from each partner's family.

1. Those Who Understand Family History Are Not Doomed to Repeat It

There is an old adage that those who do not study history are condemned to repeat it. We are not that pessimistic and have seen individuals and couples spontaneously correct interactional patterns which were dysfunctional. Nevertheless, when couples work with us, they are continually working with issues in their families of origin. There is no blame placed on the family by the therapists, although many adults go through a period of intense anger and blaming as they realize that some of the problems they now experience were created before they knew any better. It is part of our work to assist each member of a couple in understanding the legacy received by the family in relation to values, ethics, communication styles, and gender role issues.

After individuals better understand their legacy—through direct discussion with family members, through bringing photos into therapy sessions, and through rethinking old assumptions—we enable the couple to make new and—hopefully—more effective choices in the areas they want the change (Stone, 1988). These changes impact not only on their marriage and their own generation, but also on their children's generation and, at times, on the parental generation.

2. Current Couple Conflicts Always Relate to Issues from Each Partner's Family

Despite its cynicism, we occasionally paraphrase a quip by Carl Whitaker and tell couples that there is no such thing as marriage. There are only emissaries from two families of origin, fighting for control of the next generation. After laughing at the ridiculous nature of this situation, couples often are able to put a conflict into a reality frame which enables them to problem-solve in a new way.

RESISTANCE AS AN ALLY IN THERAPEUTIC CHANGE

From work done with Olga Silverstein at the Ackerman Family Therapy Institute, as well as from related readings in strategic family therapy, we have come to value the concept of a dialectic between stability and change (Keeney & Ross, 1985). We believe that therapists need to introduce new elements into the change process gradually, testing to see if the couple is ready for increased change. Therapists also need to realize that couples will naturally work to maintain stability and balance by remaining unchanged. Resistance is not an enemy in psychotherapy, but rather a natural occurrence in the process of change for individuals, families, couples, and groups.

We see resistance as a friend to therapy, not a foe, because it represents the couple's need to remain stable and predictable. We believe that a solid therapeutic alliance between therapist and clients redirects resistance rather than doing battle with it. Resistance in therapy has a number of phases (Coché, 1990) and an awareness of the process of working with resistance enables the therapist to have a cognitive set towards it which allows a tracking of the phase of the resistance and, thereby, a control over moving the process along. After the initial consult, one can see three phases.

1. Joining and reframing.   The task here is to enable the couple to feel a connection with the therapist at the same time that the therapist sets limits on the boundaries of their experience together. Whitaker calls this phase the battle for structure (Neill & Kniskern, 1982).

2. Enabling people to feel deeply their fear of not changing.   People change when there is nothing left to do. The skill at this stage is basically to offer support and listening skills while the couple worry that they may be so stuck that even couples therapy, and even couples group therapy, will not help.

3. Turning the corner.   After enabling people to connect intimately with their fear of not changing and to join others who are able to listen to them and to echo the themes they discuss, a freeing-up usually happens in relation to the issue which has proved frustrating. It is as if a therapeutic corner is turned. But, as one corner is turned, the resistance dance begins again, for the next therapeutic corner is, indeed, just around the corner.

INCORPORATING LISTENING AND COMMUNICATION SKILLS

Some of the couples work is very basic, especially if a couple has had no therapy experience as a unit. Often, paradoxically, years spent in individual therapy by one partner has calcified the reality frame at the level of "It's all his/her problem." Getting couples unstuck often means teaching adults how to know what they feel, how to listen actively to someone else, and how to communicate clearly. Part of our assessment procedure is an assessment of these factors.

We see the process as one of learning a new language. A couple must start where the skills of the least skilled partner reside. They will proceed at the pace inherent in their interest in learning the language of self and couples communication, and at the pace of their natural intelligence. Some people are more naturally skilled than others; within a couple, it is most frequently the woman who has more natural skills.

Following are four useful steps in increasing the fluency in couples communication:

1. Teach partners to recognize what they feel.
2. Teach couples to listen actively to the partner.

3. Teach partners to communicate clearly and carefully.

4. Teach couples to respectfully negotiate differences.

These steps in increasing the fluency of couples in communicating with one another are adapted from schools of humanistic psychotherapy (Wexler & Rice, 1974; Rogers, 1957; Truax & Carkhuff, 1967) and from Satir's (1967, 1988) work in couples communication.

Steps one and two comprise a kind of basic language course in feelings and empathy. If needed, we train people to learn how to deal with what they feel by teaching a four-step model to identify the feeling physiologically, to label it with words, to consider the alternatives in acting on the feeling, and, finally, to handle the feeling in a preplanned manner. We may even hand out a "crib sheet" of about 300 words which name feelings in the English language. Although the sheet began as a spoof on humanistic psychotherapy, we have found that some very task-oriented clients find the assistance very helpful and have been known to carry the sheet with them for those situations in which the word describing the feeling escapes the partner who wishes to communicate more effectively with the spouse.

After we can see that people know how they feel and can describe it, we teach them empathy skills. We do exercises in active listening in couples work or in the group. The progress in active listening becomes part of the work partners do if communication is a problem in the marriage. Couples tell us that this very basic human skill is a very powerful added bonus in their marriage, since it gives them a more effective way to discuss a variety of issues.

The third step, teaching couples to communicate clearly and carefully, comprises structured exercises in the couples group. We borrow exercises from Satir (1988), modify them, or make up new ones to fit the group at hand. This step is much better done in a small group because the feedback from other members greatly enhances the learning process for both listeners and communicators.

Once the other three skills have been developed, couples have a foundation on which they can negotiate, with mutual respect, differences along the many dimensions that adults disagree about in an intimate relationship. Here we borrow more from the business community in teaching negotiating skills and create exercises which fit the group as needed.

These four basic steps cut across the usual areas of trouble (sex, money, children, etc.) and provide process tools by which couples can build stronger relationships within themselves, and between themselves and other group members. This kind of skill building increases the likelihood that, after therapy is completed, the marriage will be one in which change is maintained in the desired direction because the tools to maintain the change have been internalized.

GENDER ISSUES IN COUPLES DEVELOPMENT

Much of the clinical work in couples and group psychotherapy is founded on concepts based in general systems theory as applied to adult male and female development. The field of adult development as a source of theory and research has played a central role in thinking about members of our couples as individuals and in partnership with one another. These related fields of adult male development and adult female development have yielded clinically valuable findings for conceptualizing and treating our couples. A great deal of the work in these fields has been concerned with gender differences in developmental phases within adulthood for men and for women.

Levinson and coauthors (1978) and Vaillant (1977) added to our understanding of the centrality of career identity for adult males, while Gilligan (1982) and Miller (1976) began to alert us to the value of exploring further women's ways of knowing, feeling, and experiencing what life brings. Work by Judith Coché on female therapists as clients (1984) and on the impact of roles on family development (1980) indicated the centrality of these concepts in an earlier clinical formulation. Current thinking and writing continues to explore gender issues in couples and group work with ongoing enthusiasm. These ongoing shifts in our knowledge base as social scientists were soon reflected in clinical guidelines in gender-sensitive family therapy (McGoldrick, Anderson & Walsh, 1989; Walters, Carter, Papp & Silverstein, 1988; Coché, 1984). The result of this remarkable deluge in extending our reality frame to encompass contemporary views of role and gender in marriage have been incorporated into our work with relief and enthusiasm.

Clinical interventions are still in the formative stage, but include the simplest language-based intervention. Each time someone refers to an adult female as a "girl," a therapist intercedes with, "Do you mean woman?" For couples like Leo and Penny and Morris and Leslie, the simplicity of this intervention belies its power. Morris has spent much time in therapy railing against being corrected for referring to Leslie as a "girl," asserting that this is merely a term of endearment. Leslie thinks otherwise.

One couples group has made the gender role theme primary in their group work. At the beginning of the group three of the four couples referred to women as girls. They suffered from isolated marriages in which the male was sole supporter and was working 70-hour work weeks. The fourth couple was much less traditional in their handling of gender-based marital roles: When Amy got pregnant, the couple decided that she would work after the baby was born, while Paul stayed home to attend to infant care. The conflict, confusion, and tension in the group created by this "odd" couple in relation to the other three proved a remarkable catalyst for change in all four couples. Amy became less militant and angry with the traditional patterns espoused by Ellis, Jack, and Guy. Tess, Deirdre, and Jaime began to look to Amy as a role model for a different kind of intimacy between males and females.

To summarize, any therapist's couples work is a rich and dynamic tapestry, woven from one's philosophical beliefs and values, one's personal and professional experience with couples therapy, one's previous training in therapy, and the wish to give couples practical skills within a highly abstract philosophical framework. Within this model, the philosophical framework presented here is based on concepts integrated by the authors from the fields of existential and strategic family therapy, as well as psychodynamic and humanistic ideas.

5.
Building Cohesiveness in Couples and Groups

Be more careful of each other and more careful of yourselves in dealing with each other.

—Penny to Morris and Leslie

Intimacy between members is the hallmark of a cohesive unit. A group in which members can share important aspects of their personal lives has to be cohesive in order to make such sharing possible. As the group members become more open in their honest disclosure of deeply felt emotions or details of their private lives, their group becomes increasingly cohesive. The mutual reinforcement of sharing and cohesiveness is one of the distinguishing properties of a well-functioning group.

The same is true for couples. The cohesive marital unit is one in which partners openly share intimate notions, thoughts, feelings, memories. As more of this sharing occurs, partners feel close and strongly bonded to each other. Where there are secrets and a refusal to let the other participate in one's inner thoughts and feelings there are always distance and isolation between the partners. The same circularity between cohesiveness and honesty can be observed in couples as in groups. It is for this reason that we shall discuss the issue of cohesiveness in the group simultaneously with that in a couple.

Cohesiveness can be described as the degree to which the group is attractive to its members (Sherif & Sherif, 1969). Phrased differently, cohesiveness is the degree of the desire of the members to be in the group. Thus, cohesiveness is measurable by the expressions of the group members regarding how much they enjoy the group and are glad to be in it. Conversely, a group in which members complain a great deal is not likely to be very cohesive. A less obvious yet still useful yardstick is the eagerness with which people come to group. Are they on time or early, are they willing to go through particular hardships like bad weather, car trouble, etc. in order to attend? Finally, the sentiment of not wanting to leave group (especially in the later sessions) can give an indication of cohesiveness.

In this way, cohesiveness, which is sometimes seen as some mysterious force which holds the group together, becomes much less mysterious. The presence of this force is noticeable in a group and the leader is well advised to stay tuned to its manifestations and to any indications of its absence.

ISOMORPHISM IN COUPLES AND GROUPS

The principle of isomorphism states that in related systems similar processes will occur on different levels. This principle is particularly applicable to cohesiveness in couples and groups. The partners in a couple struggling with issues of intimacy and openness are likely to show a fear of self-disclosure in the group as well. As the group teaches them to take more risks and to share their feelings, they also learn to do so in their marriage.

There is no sense in telling people that self-disclosure is risk-free: There always is the possibility that one's thoughts might be misunderstood or "used against" the speaker at some later time. Instead of teaching the group members denial and a blithe pretension that this risk does not exist, the leaders and the group as a whole need to teach the members that the gain in intimacy, warmth, and closeness is worth the risk and that partners can learn to treat one another's self-disclosures with respect and care.

WHY IS COHESIVENESS IMPORTANT IN GROUPS?

Cohesiveness is crucial to effective group functioning (Nobler, 1986). Research in group dynamics and group psychotherapy has shown that cohesive groups are more effective in reaching their stated goals. Cohesive groups foster not only more openness, but also more altruism and helping behaviors. In turn, the increase in altruism and openness enhances cohesiveness.

Group psychotherapy outcome ultimately depends on these factors. If clients are to benefit from their group or couples therapy experience, it has to be one in which members explore their thoughts, feelings, and beliefs in some depth. People will do this only if they feel a sufficient degree of safety and if they truly want to be present in the group.

SIX BUILDING BLOCKS OF COHESIVE GROUPS

In order to enhance and safeguard the cohesiveness of a group, the leader can employ a number of strategies which will be described later in this chapter. Before discussing those, however, it is worthwhile to examine a number of group properties which are typical of a cohesive group and which will emerge if leader and group members cooperate in bringing these to life. Although the leader has a great deal to do with the generation of these building blocks of cohesiveness, ultimately the group must participate in the task and must curtail covert or unconscious efforts to block cohesiveness. This is harder than it sounds.

Following are the six major building blocks of cohesive groups:

1. The safe harbor of the group
2. Acceptance
3. Assumption that the power to change is within the couple or the group
4. Modeling of honesty
5. Universality
6. Humor

1. The Safe Harbor of the Group

In order to risk self-disclosure, group members have to feel reasonably safe. They have to have some sense that the other members, and especially their spouse, will not attack them for what they disclose and will not use the information against them.

> Jaime and Ellis joined the group because Jaime believed that Ellis had taken advantage of her goodwill. Ellis was angry and accused Jaime of being continually critical of his ability as a lover, as a father and son-in-law, and as a decent human being. Attempts at discussion only drove the couple further apart. Mutual trust was limited to his ability to earn a living and her ability to be lovely and entertaining.
>
> When they entered the group each was quick to feel betrayed by the other if the partner attempted to describe the content of a fight. The group became an extremely valuable resource for both. Jaime could hear from other women what she was unable to hear from Ellis. Ellis respected and especially listened to one man in the group, because he believed that this man could understand him.

One strategy which contributes to the members' feeling that the group is a safe harbor is the clear explication of the group policies at the beginning of the group experience. The rules regarding confidentiality especially help the members to know that their contributions will be handled with care. In this atmosphere, the leader will be able to encourage risk taking and self-disclosure. The sharing of actual here-and-now emotions—for example, the anxiety felt by most in the first session—will help members to understand that such sharing is not only safe but even contributes to a discovery of a shared emotion and thus to greater cohesiveness.

2. Acceptance

Related to the concept of self-disclosure is the concept of acceptance. People in the group need to feel that they are being accepted by their group members. This does not mean that the other people in the group have to unconditionally accept or approve of everything the member says. On the contrary, members can be and often are quite annoyed, irritated, or perturbed about a certain behavior that is being described or shown in the group. Hopefully, however, there is still a basic acceptance of that person as a group member. The thought should come across that the group still wants this person in its midst even though he or she may show some very antagonistic or even socially unacceptable behaviors in and outside of the group.

The main strategy for the group leaders is to prevent criticism from becoming a dominant tone in the group. Leaders can help members to learn to distinguish between constructive feedback and taking potshots. While criticism of people's actions may at times be desirable and necessary, it should not permeate the group to the point where people become afraid of self-disclosing or interaction with others. Sometimes, this requires giving people instruction in such a way that the feedback does not come across as a moral condemnation.

> In one of our groups, Jack was a very active and helpful participant, frequently commenting on the thoughts and narratives presented by others in the group. However, Jack's comments were frequently given in a very stern "fire and brimstone" tone. He was a devoutly religious man who had very high moral standards for himself, his family, his employees, and the others in the group. The leaders had to work diligently to teach Jack the difference between constructive feedback and moral condemnation.

> He struggled with this for quite a while, believing that it was his duty to tell others the ethical implications of their behaviors. Knowing that his moralistic stance posed a danger to the group which could easily become overshadowed by the fire and brimstone, as had Jack's family, the leaders persisted and eventually succeeded in softening some, though not all, of Jack's rigidity.

3. Assumption That the Power to Change is Within the Couple or the Group

People come into couples therapy because they are in pain and want to change. Naturally, there is a concomitant resistance to making changes. It is the task of the therapist to facilitate those forces within each person that are struggling for constructive change. In doing so, the therapist has to avoid the fantasy that he/she can actively change a person. The same goes for the group. The impetus to make changes and strive towards greater intimacy and honesty is already present in the group, though the group is also laced with fear. If the leader can deal with this resistance to change in a creative manner, the group can make changes which will have their parallel in the members' personal lives and marriages.

Most importantly, there are ways in which the leaders communicate either the belief that the power to change lies in the group or the opposite fantasy of omnipotence, that is, the belief that the leaders can produce the change. If the group is convinced that it has the power to change with merely some assistance from the leader, a more cohesive and actively working group will result.

4. Modeling of Honesty

In order for the group to be cohesive, leaders must be honest with each other and with the group. Any kind of falsehood will be reacted to very negatively by the group. If the leaders communicate to the group that it has the power to change its rules in a democratic fashion, but then block all the changes the group wants to make, an atmosphere of resentment and mistrust will arise quickly. Likewise, the group will be very distrustful of co-leaders who interact with one another in an unreal or phoney way.

Clearly, the matter of honesty between the leaders is as important in a couples group as it is in a couple. Pittman (1989) writes about the model of honesty as the foundation in a marriage. We agree that honesty is especially necessary when it is painful to the couple, and especially painful when the couple is a co-therapy team afraid to alienate or insult a colleague who is also a co-therapist.

5. Universality

Groups work better together if participants know that others in the group are going through experiences similar to theirs. Knowing that one is not alone in facing a difficult marital problem helps the couple feel at home in the group. The group support enables couples to work hard at finding a solution to their problems, frequently with the help of those in the group who are struggling with similar issues. The universality in a couples group begins with problems in a marriage . . . all couples have them. All couples have to deal at some time with certain marital issues which we call, "The Universals of Marriage."

The other kind of universality which also greatly contributes to cohesiveness is the common struggle with a current group problem. Whether this is the anxiety at the beginning of the group, or the discomfort at the point of a group crisis, or any other kind of joint group struggle, the knowledge that others in the group are troubled by the same problem and are equally intent to work it through helps the members feel more committed to the group.

6. Humor

Just as much as a group needs sadness and tears of honest confrontation of difficult problems, it also needs the comic relief from humor and laughter (Bloch, Browning & McGrath, 1983). Frequently, a couple is helped by a hilarious parody of their incessant repetitive fights more than by repetitive confrontation of the same absurd interaction. However, it is important to watch out that the parody and humor, even though biting, are not disrespectful, and do not give a couple the impression that their problem is not being taken seriously. "Accidents" in this direction happen. A couple which has a mirror held up to it in a comical way occasionally take offense initially. However, if the group can simultaneously communicate its caring for this couple, the "bite" will be effective and the humor can have its therapeutic effect. Such an experience frequently turns out to be a strong cohesiveness builder.

Humor is also a central ingredient in many of the structured experiences. A good number of these can be successfully conducted only if the group members maintain a sense of humor about them. If they do, they experience a very positive and enjoyable way to learn something important. When one of our groups did the Noah's Ark exercise (described earlier), peals of laughter greeted the herons fluttering through the room, the zebras cuddling with each other, and the lion and lioness stalking each other. Group members talked about this exercise for quite a while, reiterating how much they had enjoyed the activity but also how much they had learned about themselves and the other couples while doing so.

LEADERSHIP SKILLS THAT ENHANCE COHESIVENESS

A frequent concern of the professionals attending our workshops centers around the skills involved in building cohesiveness. Here the skills of the leaders can be doubly useful, for, while they concentrate on building a cohesive working group, they create a therapeutic community which simultaneously models the qualities of a successfully intimate and cohesive marriage.

Following are some important group leadership skills which enhance cohesiveness:

1. Communicating the leaders' belief in the group
2. Prepositioning
3. Employing structured exercises

4. Enabling group celebrations and teaming
5. Distributing leaders' attention among all couples
6. Encouraging constructive self-disclosure

1. Leaders Communicate Their Belief in the Group

Leaders demonstrate their belief in the group in a variety of ways. If they go out of their way for the group, make sure that the group begins and ends on time, manage to get to the group despite weather and other calamities, and help members to overcome their difficulties in getting to the group, they are sending a message: This group is important to us. If, conversely, they cancel for unimportant sounding reasons, come late, or appear disinterested, group members will follow their lead and develop a careless attitude about the group. Even as early as in the preparation for the group the leaders can sound convincing and enthusiastic or perfunctory. This early impression can swing members' attitudes and make the group seem appealing or unappealing.

2. Prepositioning . . . A Leadership Skill

For years, we have informally referred to the connecting of people in the group as "prepositioning," a term Judith concocted early in our training. The group leaders formulate connecting terms (like the prepositions in grammatical structures) which demonstrate to the members how their issues are related to those of others in the group. Similarities and differences, transferences, subgroupings, and hierarchical relationships—all these can be highlighted to help members feel the invisible lines between themselves and others in the group.

For this, some groups need no help from their leaders; it comes naturally to them and they virtually sparkle with frequent expressions like, "That's exactly what we do, too!" Other groups need lots of help to see the connections. Here the leaders' knowledge of the couples in the group comes into play and formulating the prepositions turns into an art form. Prepositioning can take the form of merely pointing out similarities in the problems two or more couples may be struggling with, or can rely on more sophisticated strategies like helping people see the complementarity in their mutual struggles. In the latter case, a person may be struggling with an issue represented by a group member who responds in kind.

Harry was a Jewish businessmen who joined the couples group after 45 years of married struggle with Rita. Will was a professional, age 34, whose father had died when Will was 16, leaving him emotionally orphaned. At first the entire group, upset by Harry's casual and abrasive manner in dealing both with Rita and with the human problems in the other couples, attempted to confront Harry, to get him to "see the light." This increased Harry's militancy and further isolated him from the group. Judith gently pointed out the similarities between both men, both successful, both courageous, both Jewish, both businessmen. She even mentioned that Harry could be valuable to Will, since Will desperately missed the opportunity to learn from his own Dad about how to be a man. This prepositioning softened the antagonism towards Harry and framed his experience as valuable and within the interests of the group.

3. Employing Structured Exercises

We find that structured exercises which promote cohesiveness can be of special value early in the life of a group. This can be done in a variety of ways. Research in group relations (e.g. Sherif & Sherif, 1969) has shown that the cohesiveness of a group can be enhanced by purposeful common activities. We have found that sharing, fun, and deep emotional experiences have the most power.

Promote sharing. In the beginning stages of a couples group, exercises which encourage people to share data about themselves in a somewhat formalized way speed up the process of getting to know the other people in the group. Going-around activities are the most natural way to do so and everyone in the group takes a turn to respond to instructions like: "Introduce yourself," or "Tell us what it is you want to get out of this group. How can the group help you?"

Another sharing exercise comes about quite naturally. In the second group session we ask couples to share with the group what they wrote in response to specific questions on the Couples Assessment form. Starting with a round of positive messages ("What was it that initially attracted you to your partner?"), members find it easier to move on to the more painful questions like: "What are the major issues in the marriage now?" Giving each person a chance to present his/her view of the marriage encourages self-disclosure, helps members to get to know each other, and avoids monopolization by the more verbal members.

Promote fun. Having a common enjoyable learning experience greatly enhances a group's sense of cohesiveness. Conducting an enjoyable exercise merely "for the fun of it" is a risky venture. People may enjoy the exercise at first (thus it will increase cohesiveness), but they may soon believe that they are wasting their time and that the group is not addressing serious issues. On the other hand, planning a group exercise which packages some significant learning in a delightful shell not only deepens the learning but also creates a common group memory which the group will occasionally remember as a part of its history.

One unforgettable exercise occurred because a number of the members of one group loved ballroom dancing (Skip and Nell, Lena and Jared), while others in the same group (Karl and Randy) were awkwardly uncomfortable with their bodies and with dancing with their partners in public. We obtained a tape of a 1940s Fred Astaire-type music and invited each couple to dance a quick step and a slow dance in the center of the room while the other couples sat and observed the dancers. The awkwardness became less painful when shared with trusted group friends, while the elegant dancers modelled for the group the beauty of a couple moving skillfully together. Besides being fun for all and providing an opportunity for hearty laughter, the exercise stimulated a group discussion of physical affection and sexuality.

Common moving experiences. As the group matures, members will share more and more profound feelings. Love, hate, pain, and dread are openly discussed; narratives of painful experiences punctuate a session. Frequently, the telling of experiences is not planned at all, but when it happens, it is a sign of the trust, maturity, and cohesiveness of the group.

One night, when a group was still in a beginning stage, Leo and Penny, embarking on their second group year, were unexpectedly absent because Leo suffered a sudden but mild heart attack between sessions two and three. In session four, Penny and Leo returned and gave a sobering and moving account of the attack, its prelude, and its aftermath. The group listened in stunned silence to the narrative and to the couple's appreciation of the card which the group had made as a collective get-well wish. This led to a general group discussion in which several members shared experiences dealing with moments of utter terror at the thought of losing the partner. A mood came over the group which—at least for a time—put a lot of the petty arguments (which frequently preoccupy a group in its early stages) into a new perspective.

Usually such sharing happens later in the group year. In this case it happened early in the group because of the heart attack, and had a very beneficial effect on the group. If this happens too early and the group is not ready, there is the possibility of a backlash: People may temporarily become less open because the level of disclosure and honesty was frightening. This danger is not too serious, however. Given the choice, it is better to err in the direction of too much rather than too little sharing. The more common complaint of groups in the early-to-middle stage is that people are too polite and not self-disclosing enough.

4. Enabling Group Celebrations

Many groups will spontaneously celebrate birthdays, anniversaries, births, etc. Sometimes, people will bring in food and in that way let the celebrant know that the group cares about the special occasion and wants to share in the joy. Celebrations should, however, not be forced. We are sparing with our own initiatives in this direction lest they send a message that it is the group's task to have parties. We encourage the festivity if it is initiated by the group and is kept in a frame which does not detract from the therapeutic goal of the group.

5. Leaders Distribute Attention Among All Couples

A group in which people feel that one person, couple, or segment of the group is getting too much attention will soon become disgruntled about this situation. Whether this arises from the activities of a monopolizer or because the leaders (perhaps unconsciously) favor some participants over others, it is a phenomenon that definitely undermines cohesiveness.

At times, some unevenness arises because a couple is in a kind of permanent crisis and appears to need a lot of attention, perhaps to keep from separating or divorcing. At these times, the leaders need to be particularly watchful. At first, the group is likely to rally around this couple, thereby rewarding its crisis-laden style of interacting, and the group rally becomes a cohesiveness-builder. After a few sessions, however, the group will become dissatisfied and the members' desire to be there will drop sharply (see Chapter 6 for more on this topic). At that point, the leaders need to make special efforts to bring the whole group together and to reengage the rest without disregarding the couple in crisis. Sometimes, a frank discussion about this situation is the best strategy.

6. Encouraging Constructive Self-Disclosure

Research in the field of patient self-disclosure has shown that a positive tone of the self-disclosure is more therapeutically effective than public self-criticism, especially if this torture is prolonged (Coché, Polikoff & Cooper, 1980). It is sometimes desirable to conduct exercises which give group members the opportunity to shine or even brag. It is certainly valuable and cohesiveness-building to occasionally focus on people's competence and to give others in the group a chance to get to know the sparkling sides of a couple as well as the less attractive ones.

Focusing on the positive in people's self-disclosures does not mean that one avoids confrontation. Where it is indicated, the leaders will still need to hold up a mirror to the group members regarding their behavior inside and outside of the group — or encourage the group to do so. That, after all, is one of the jobs of good group leaders. We are merely advising against the repetitive and therapeutically useless public self-flagellations to which depressives are especially prone. We want to encourage some enthusiastic exercises, especially early on in a group's life.

SOME FINAL CONSIDERATIONS: THE REWARDS OF COHESIVENESS

Groups which are cohesive are a pleasure to lead. Usually, they are earnest and hardworking, yet still able to have fun and an occasional good laugh. Members have a sense of purpose and feel they are participating in something which is valuable and helpful to them. Thus, they are eager to be there and get down to work.

This thought was expressed most eloquently by one of our members who in the last session of his group year was participating in a termination exercise in which we ask the group participants to think up farewell gifts for the other members (persons, couples, and group-as-a-whole). To express his affection for the group and his sense of the importance it had for him, he responded with: "I'm giving this group my gift of perfect attendance."

6.

Making the Most
of the Stages
# of Group Development

I just want to say thanks... the journey from deadness to misery has been wonderful.

— *Serge*

Groups have developmental stages very much like the stages of human development. A group has to go through certain processes which repeat themselves as a group progresses from its first meeting to a working stage of development (Bennis & Shephard, 1956; Bion, 1960; Thelen, 1954). Stages are to some degree predictable. Frequently, they have marker events by which one can tell that a group has reached a stage or is moving from one stage to the next. Stages imply that there is a certain developmental task which the group has to master. Often the atmosphere in the group will convey to the leaders that the group is struggling with such a task. Understanding these tasks and working with them maximizes the effects of the group. Thus, if a group is dealing with issues of joining and acceptance, the leader is ill-advised to focus on mutuality and intimacy in the group; those are issues which belong to later stages. Instead, it is advantageous to help the group clarify the current stage task and guide the group in its search for stage-appropriate solutions to its issues.

From our clinical work and our knowledge of the literature, we believe that there are a number of repetitive patterns which can best be understood as developmental stages (Kirschenbaum & Glinder, 1972). Our way of organizing them is, at this point, still tentative and awaiting experimental verification. However, we believe that the stage sequence as described here provides a useful way of looking at group development and can help in understanding group phenomena which would otherwise be quite puzzling. This sequential course assumes that the group is closed ended and lasts an adequate number of sessions; thus, it will not be accurate for a short-term couples group or for an open-ended one.

Throughout the life of a group a dialectical dance occurs between the forces of therapeutic progress and those of stability or resistance. No one yields old patterns gladly, be they ever so painful. Therefore, resistance is a major issue for the duration of the year. Interestingly enough, however, resistance takes on different forms in the different developmental stages. In the following discussion, we will take a look at these forms of resistance as we discuss the stages one by one.

STAGES IN GROUP DEVELOPMENT

Following are five major stages in the development of the group:

1. Joining
2. The beginning working phase
3. Group crisis/dissatisfaction
4. The intensive working phase
5. Termination

1. Joining

The first phase of the beginning couples group we call the *Joining Stage*. In the first few sessions, people in the group show much concern with acceptance and fear of not being accepted. A great deal of the anxiety experienced by people in the first session is reflective of a fear of being rejected. Some of the surprising behaviors shown by some group members in the first session can be explained as new members' attempts to cope with this anxiety as best they can. Of course, since people under stress tend to overutilize their preferred defense mechanism, the talkative person chats more and the shy person even less in the first session and people may, in fact, end up showing themselves from their least favorable side in the first session. In other words, a member frequently demonstrates the areas in the self which need work through the member's introduction of self in the group.

The first stage is also marked by much social politeness and propriety, something we have termed "social lubrication." Couples behave in the way they have learned when they get together with other couples: They are more polite, more "social." Because of this, the beginning of a couples group tends to be somewhat slower than that of a non-couples group.

Another reason for the slower start is that individuals who come to the group with their partner are often somewhat more reluctant to self-disclose than they would be if they were there without their spouse. The following reasons seem to contribute to this phenomenon:

(a) People may be afraid to report on certain problems in front of their partner. Many couples appear to have a silent agreement in the marriage along the lines of, "We don't wash our dirty laundry in public." Even if the "public" is their group, shame about vulnerable issues prevents self-disclosure at first.

(b) There are certain taboo topics in each couple which the partners themselves are not able to discuss even when they are alone with each other. Partners often are unaware of these taboo subjects as problems worth mentioning.

(c) No couple wants to believe they have the worst marriage in the group. Consequently, couples are rather tentative at first and when asked to tell the group what the problems are which brought them to the group, they often minimize the problem, leave out important aspects, or deny large chunks of the trouble. Obviously, especially in the early stage of the group, loyalty to the partner takes priority over loyalty to the group.

While that is still likely to be true in later stages, a group member will later on be more able to adhere to a group norm of openness even when honesty feels disloyal to the partner. Therefore, a group needs to do some work on this issue early on. Self-disclosure needs to become a group norm which is understood as beneficial to the marriage, so that even if it *feels* like disloyalty to the partner, group members can offer acceptance and understanding. Leaders need to distinguish for the group that group loyalty does not supersede couple loyalty, but that the couple benefits from a group norm of self-disclosure.

> During the initial phase of a couples group, Will was the more active group participant, in part because he had been in other forms of group psychotherapy (while his wife Denise had not) and understood the value of openness and risk taking. After a few sessions, someone in the group pointed out that he had a funny habit of always throwing a quick sideways glances at Denise which seemed to indicate his concern that she might disapprove of what he was about to say. When made aware of this, Will was able to acknowledge this concern and to talk openly about his fear of her feelings of betrayal. Other group members chimed in with similar hesitations about being disloyal to their partners. The discussion which ensued helped not only Will and Denise but others in the group as well.

Resistance in the early stage often takes on the quality of, "Even if you don't agree with me, stay by my side in group," or, "If you love me you'll agree with me in group." The group at this point is rarely sophisticated enough to deal with this kind of collusion by couples. Therefore, the leaders have to spearhead the movement to confront it.

Another phenomenon of the first group phase is that of dependency on the leaders (Bennis & Shephard, 1956; Bion, 1960; Thelen, 1954). Groups at this juncture have to establish their basic interactional norms. Frequently, they are not sure which of the norms they are permitted to set for themselves and which are simply prescribed by the leaders. Thus, they will look to the leaders for guidance to a considerable degree. Our response to these dependency issues is often to discuss the phenomenon out loud, so that the group is able to understand that its dependency needs will have to be met by spouses and other members rather than by the leaders.

The first phase is also characterized by ambivalence over being in the group. It is not unusual for a new group member to have joined merely because the spouse insisted, perhaps even with a veiled threat that signing up is the last chance for the marriage. Naturally, a person joining the group under these circumstances is there under duress and may participate only perfunctorily or put up active resistance. A variation of this phenomenon is one or both partners in a couple with the belief that only one of them has a problem.

In this example of a couple who agree that this is the wife's problem, Erik reviews his answers to the couple's questionnaire:[*]

Judith: Looking at your questionnaire again, can you tell us major problems in your relationship, and can you tell us how you have worked within the couples group to try to solve some of those problems?

Erik: Well, . . . Nan's undependable. Before joining the group, I tried to limit my expectations, but she resents that. She solves problems very slowly, which is what brought us to the group. I've tried to discuss it with her but she always thinks I'm trying to solve her problems and she resents it, so the whole thing just becomes more entrenched.

When I was growing up, I always had the feeling that my father wasn't really involved in his marriage, that whatever my mother wanted was what got done. The women in my family ruled supreme, especially my grandmother. The men tried to please the women, regardless of cost. Loyalty to the family was the supreme obligation. And that's really kind of what I'm doing here. I came to this out of a sense of loyalty to Nan. I really don't think that I had that big a problem. I was in a system that was working until Nan started pointing out everything that was wrong with it, for her.

---

[*]Transcript from the videotape, *Techniques in Couples Group Psychotherapy.*

The hesitancy over becoming a fully committed member is also related to the above-mentioned anxiety over acceptance. New members of any group are worried about being accepted by others. This phenomenon exacerbates the problems described above: Members become reluctant to self-disclose ("If I let them know this about me they might not like me"), they feel leader-dependency, they actively deny that they have a problem. After all, "If there is nothing wrong with me, there is less self-esteem to lose and if the group rejects me it will not be much of a loss." In order to move on to the next level and get some meaningful work done, the group has to find workable solutions to three issues: self-disclosure, dependency, and membership. In terms of self-disclosure, members must agree that it is in each couple's best interest to talk freely about painful and embarrassing personal and marital issues.

In terms of dependency, members have to learn that the leader is not there to provide answers, but that solutions to the pain which brought the couple to the group have to emerge from the members themselves (Bion, 1960). Finally, in terms of membership, a commitment to the group by all members is necessary. Partners who entered the couples group believing that they joined only because their spouse had a problem have to be introduced to a more systemic view of their pain. Couples must begin to understand the interactional problems of the marriage in systems terms in order to effectively improve communication skills, as discussed in Chapter 4.

2. Beginning Working Phase (and Prelude to Crisis)

We call this the beginning working phase because members have found a preliminary solution to the tasks of stage one and have settled in to work on marital problems. Frequently, it is the impatience of those group members who are already fluent in the language of family systems work through earlier therapy that moves the group to this stage. These members settle the self-disclosure issue simply by "taking the plunge" and modeling openness for the others, which catalyzes the group.

Serge entered psychotherapy a few years ago to learn from the mistakes he had made with Suzanne, the wife he was leaving. He learned a great deal about the choices he made with women. After two years in individual therapy and in group therapy with Judith, he ended therapy to "live life." Therapist and patient both predicted, at that time, that when Serge met his next bride, some couples work would be advantageous to work on communication skills in intimate relationships.

Serge brought Lisa for a couples consultation at the time of their engagement. All parties decided not to interrupt the blissful state both were in, since no emotional pain was evident. Rather, all decided to wait to see what would develop after marriage. Five years later, Serge and

Lisa returned to marital therapy to work on the same kinds of emotional withdrawal during anger which had plagued Serge in his earlier marriage. The same year, they joined the couples group, ready to work.

The group that year consisted of couples new to therapy and reluctant to move quickly. Serge became impatient, and, just one month after the first group meeting, told Judith he wanted to drop out of the group. He told Lisa in the same week, to her astonishment, that he might be leaving the marriage as well. Judith told the couple, who were in excruciating emotional pain, to attend the next group meeting and discuss both issues with their group.

Serge dutifully told the group how polite this group was compared to his group from a decade before. He said that he and Lisa had no time to wait while people made pleasant and friendly comments. Lisa said she was in agony and believed the marriage to be hanging in the balance. They needed real help fast. The group knew that the couple were echoing statements from the leaders like, "This group is frightened to become more direct and honest with one another." Members rallied to help this couple, whom they had quickly come to like and to respect. The group bounced into the initial working phase within its third session and, in retrospect, looks upon this session as a key to its development. Lisa and Serge were buoyed at this juncture by the honest and safe community of couples which they had asked to help them.

One of the hallmarks of this stage is what might be called, "moving from couple identity to personal identity." Members, who at first were seen by the others in the group merely as partners in a couple, begin to emerge as individuals with their own style and problems. While this is very useful in the process of getting to know each other, the leaders have to be watchful that group members do not take sides in the marriage by seeing one partner in the couple as the source of the problem. The systemic view the therapists present in Chapter 4 is essential to countering this form of marital scapegoating.

Resistance to group movement at this stage is often a symbolic expression of projected dissatisfactions of a couple with each other. There is always a grain of truth in the complaint of a couple about the group, but this blame process is reflective of the unhappiness in the couple and often of their tendency to project blame in the marriage. For example, while Will and Denise criticized the group for being too polite and moving too slowly, they looked at each other for permission to speak within the group and each blamed the other for being too polite in dealing with marital conflict.

The unstructured section in this phase of the group is marked by a couple opening the session by asking the group for help with a recent marital crisis. Others join in by sharing their opinions and feelings on the matter, by giving advice, or by reporting on their handling of similar problems. Since it is still early in the group, a good deal of information is shared in this phase (family constellations, children, family of origin, parents, jobs). These data are significant and necessary for the group in order to understand the particular life situation of a couple. For the leaders, this level of sharing can feel less meaningful than the kind of work that goes on in the later phases.

Furthermore, in some groups, a particular couple may repeatedly open the session with an account of yet another quarrel, reflecting merely a variation on a theme; yet, because of the early developmental phase in the group, the group has not yet developed skills to deal with members who monopolize. Likewise, the partners are not yet able to work out the underlying conflict in a more definitive manner. Here, leader intervention can be critical in preventing monopolizing and scapegoating.

> Morris and Leslie were what we call mutual blamers. Morris blamed Leslie and Leslie blamed Morris . . . for just about everything. Each came by the tendency honestly. Morris had been criticized by a harsh father. Leslie grew up hearing her mother blame her Dad's drinking for the ills of the family. All fights, regardless of content, had the same boring, long-winded, frustrating melody, and the group quickly tired of Morris and Leslie's song. Although this new group did not know how to solve this problem, they did know that they, as a group, could tolerate it no longer.
>
> To prevent scapegoating, we suggested that other group members stop trying to help Morris and Leslie with the content of the arguments and concentrate instead on interrupting the mutual blame process. We explained how mutual blame in a couple operates to rob the marriage of vital energy and suggested that the group could help by expressing their boredom and by reminding the couple when the mutual blame was occurring in the group. The group learned both how to work with mutual blame and how to get the group unstuck, with leader assistance.

Thus, although the group is actually working from the first minutes of its existence, in the earlier phases much of its interaction sounds tentative, superficial, and perhaps repetitive to leaders used to cohesive groups. To the new members, the group feels like a working group; however, the more experienced members and leaders know how much more a group is capable of. Thus, the experienced members are often the first to become dissatisfied and restless. Even if there is no couple returning for the second year who express the dissatisfaction, there are always one or two people or couples who are eager and able to work at greater depth. They become displeased with what is going on in the beginning group.

Most of the time the disgruntlement is directed at "the group" and is expressed, with apologies and embarrassment, as a vague impatience with the group's seeming politeness, superficiality, and repetitiveness. At other times, the dissatisfaction is directed at a specific member or couple in a typical scapegoating maneuver. Leaders need to take care to avoid scapegoating by teaching the group about its whole-group processes.

Finally, the dissatisfaction may be directed at the leaders (Bennis & Shephard, 1956). Being still somewhat dependent, members expect leaders to take responsibility for the group and to push the group to work at a greater depth by preventing the superficial rehashing of marital spats. In a typically counterdependent move, the group turns on the leaders and the stage is set for a crisis. This kind of stage-dependent crisis occurs also in individual (non-couple) psychotherapy groups (Agazarian & Peters, 1981; Rutan & Stone, 1984).

It is necessary to evaluate the degree to which the group is justified in blaming the leaders for the lack of depth at this point. As discussed earlier, some degree of superficiality is unavoidable. The group, after all, is still in an early phase and the level of self-disclosure necessary for successful group work is still very difficult to reach and maintain. However, the therapists have considerable power in determining the measure of superficiality they allow. If there are complaints about the way the group is being run, there is always some wisdom in listening to the feedback before automatically diagnosing the problem as purely developmental.

3. Crisis, Expression of Dissatisfaction

At the end of the second stage, the group goes into a crisis. What begins at first in stage two as dissatisfaction, scapegoating, or counterdependence often turns into a real battle in this phase. The onset is usually sudden: One couple may come into a session and threaten the group with dropping out if the "bullshitting" doesn't stop. Or a person suddenly loses his/her temper and noisily attacks the leaders or another member. And the battle is joined.

The fight is usually a struggle for more depth and intimacy. The people ready to move on need deeper levels of self-disclosure in order to work on painful and imbedded marital problems rather than remain at the level of superficial fights. Yet, with each important group movement there will be a countermovement. There will be some members who will resist by whatever means they can devise. They may counterattack the disgruntled attackers. They may joke around. They may pontificate about the dangers of too much openness and stepping into sensitive areas. They may deflect the attention of the group by pushing it into a seemingly important direction, yet one in which the current stage task does not get done.

> Jane had been emotionally abused by her father and had engineered a polite, stale marriage with Bertrand. Jane was an ardent feminist. At this juncture in her group, when another couple clearly wanted to do important work at a deeper level, Jane pushed the group into working on gender and power issues. She accused the males in the group of being chauvinistic. The accusation certainly seemed important, and the group followed this rather charismatic person in the direction of gender issues. However, because the group was not quite ready to handle the heat of this issue and because the directional argument over the level of group work had not yet been settled, the gender-power discussion remained vague and theoretical. And the more significant couples work others had wished for was delayed. Jane's insistence actually enabled the group to avoid work for the better part of a session.

The countermovement against greater disclosure and intimacy in a group is usually motivated by fear. While some members in the group are ready and eager to plumb greater depth, others are frightened by this prospect. They are afraid of what they might find if they were to take a harder look at their marriage and they resist. Often their fear is fueled by a vague belief that the problem of their marriage is so serious that it is insoluble and that the dissolution of the relationship is an inevitable outcome. For the therapist, it is hard to determine how much of this fear is unrealistic and how much is an awareness of a basic marital incompatibility or of a very destructive hidden fault.

Ultimately, the resolution of the crisis comes about through a dialectical process in which the people who want to move to greater depths prevail while the fears of the others are still taken into account. At times, the leaders may have to actively side with the forward-moving section of the group by commenting on the phenomenon for the group to hear. Somehow, the group needs to master the task of resolving the crisis lest it remain stuck in an untenable situation in which work gets attempted and dropped. Leader comments can be helpful. For example: "George and Eileen's impatience with Jane is actually an expression of their need to have the group work at a more intimate level."

4. The Intensive Working Phase

Once the crisis has been overcome and the group has tacitly agreed on a comfortable level of self-disclosure which creates an atmosphere in which therapeutic work can be done, the group enters its second working phase. Early in this phase the group may still be reacting to the anger of the crisis phase and may exaggerate its dedication to this new determination to work yet harder and more intimately with one another.

At the height of the crisis in her group, when several people were already complaining that the group was not working hard enough, Penny added to the complaints by vociferously admonishing the members on the slow starts of each session. Exaggerating slightly, she declared that the first 15 minutes of each session were wasted on idle chatter. She proposed that from now on people should come 10 to 15 minutes early to the group meetings and do their social chatter in the waiting room so that serious work could start as soon as the session began. To our surprise, the group agreed to the suggestion and followed it for the next several meetings. After a while, people stopped arriving early, but the groups continued to open each session quickly and productively.

At this stage, the group is very cohesive: Members express genuine liking and affection for each other, they enjoy coming to the group, lateness and complaints about how hard it is to get to group are at their lowest. The group is least resistive to serious work and one painful situation after another becomes the work of the group as members produce moving emotional experiences in these sessions.

A most striking phenomenon about this phase of the group is the intertwining of levels of personal, marital, family, and family of origin systems in the content of the group's work. Members work on couples issues, but spontaneously involve their families of origin in their explanations and narratives, or they work on a group-as-a-whole matter yet make discoveries on an individual level (through feedback from other group participants) which leads to significant personal and marital change. At this point, the group moves from level to level with ease and couples become adept at applying the learning from others to their own marital dynamics. A group working at this level is more skilled at systems therapy than most therapists trained in an individual treatment model. Leaders can literally enjoy the fruits of their and the members' labors.

Having successfully overcome the earlier struggles which, by necessity, were more superficial, the group is now able to tackle the more significant problems of power, mutuality, and intimacy in the marriages as well as in the group. The group has become central in the lives of its members. It is a time of exciting and significant and permanent personal and couple changes. Partners may find that the unspoken contract with which they entered their marriages are no longer viable and need renegotiation. Even though that process may be painful and fraught with resistance, anger, and occasional underhanded ploys, couples succeed in renegotiating past misunderstandings belatedly.

Jack and Diedre had entered their marriage with a covert understanding that he would take care of her financially. She was, in return, to park her intellect and to naively leave all important decisions to him, including finances and the furnishing of the house. At the time of their courtship, Diedre was still quite young and shy, while Jack was older, more experienced, and more outgoing, so this had seemed like a good arrangement. As Diedre matured, this unspoken agreement became increasingly intolerable to Diedre, yet the couple were unable to change it. Jack was not interested in change; he distrusted Diedre's judgment. In turn, she refrained from making decisions for fear they might turn out wrong and she would incur her husband's wrath or disapproval from other people.

In the group the two began to re-negotiate the contract but the ride became quite bumpy. Jack wanted a more satisfying marriage and was concerned over his wife's depression. However, yielding his considerable power in the family to a woman whose judgment and reasoning he did not respect was extremely difficult for him. Finding other couples in similar, albeit not quite as severe, situations helped him a great deal. Likewise, Diedre found that the support she received from the group helped her to trust her judgment more and stop her tendency to lure Jack back into the old pattern by asking him to make certain decisions alone even though they had decided earlier to make them together. Hearing from the group that they valued her judgment helped her regain faith in her considerable intellect.

The high point of the second working phase is reached at about the time of the annual workshop. Couples come to the event ready and able to work. They are usually open to new learning and, having chosen their theme for the day themselves, are willing to take risks and participate in the structured exercises with very little resistance. The resort atmosphere and the feeling of being away from the home front for a day or more (many couples stay at the seaside resort for the weekend) certainly help, but most of all it is the level of maturation the group has reached by now. At the end of the workshop day group members often feel a degree of elation. Sometimes, they wonder why we didn't have the workshop earlier in the year. Yet it is our observation that the level of cohesiveness and openness needed for a successful workshop day is usually not reached until the group has settled into the second working phase.

5. Termination

At some time soon after the annual workshop, one of the leaders reminds the group that this group will end in eight weeks. Group members usually react to this announcement with denial. The end is still weeks away and, after all, at least one couple has already announced their intent to recontract for another group year after the summer break. Ergo: "We (the group) don't have to deal with termination." Ergo: "Our group will be the first group not to end."

Despite the denial, the knowledge is there that this group will end. Even though some people may reenlist for the next group, the group as it is now will cease to exist. The members know this. After a while, the denial falls apart and the termination phase has begun.

This phase has two subphases: the pretermination rough spot and the termination itself. The first subphase is marked by some form of regression. Frequently, there is a return of some of the earlier symptoms as couples revisit some of their old trouble spots. The group can be heard moaning: "You're not fighting over *that* again are you?" However, the group has come far from its old days of projection.

Even though there is some deterioration and return of old material, the group is not usually blamed. Members now understand the concept of resistance and deal with it with more sensitivity, directness, and humor. However, the return of the old patterns is often quite poignant. It is a couple's way of signaling to the group that the partners are afraid to go on without the support from the group, that they are not sure enough of the gains they have made and are ambivalent about ending their group participation. The deterioration, at times, takes the form of acting out. A member of the group may show his/her displeasure and concern over the impending end by breaking some group rule. Usually, only one member of the couple acts out, but cannot get the other one to join in, which is quite unlike what would have occurred earlier in the group year where the partner would have felt compelled to participate out of loyalty. Furthermore, the group is likely to quickly become quite impatient with the acting out and stop it.

Nell loved her first year in the group. So did her husband of 25 years, Skip, but Skip had already become intimate enough for his own level of comfort and did not want to rejoin the group after the first year. "Enough is enough," as he put it. Nell wanted more. In May, after faithfully attending every session so far, Skip skipped out in order to go to a baseball game, not notifying the group of his absence. The group, impatient with the indirection and withdrawal which had characterized the couple's style earlier, wrote Skip a note, asking him to attend the next session and talk with them about his issues. He did. He also decided to return for a second year.

The second subphase is the termination itself. This is marked by members experiencing sadness and a feeling of loss. During this phase, recontracting becomes a major issue. Couples decide if they want to end their membership or join again for another year. They ask for feedback from the rest of the group and they report to the group on their progress made during the group year. Much of that progress is clearly visible to the group, as when a partner has stopped being condescending to his/her spouse. However, some of the progress has to do with "back home" behaviors like child rearing practices or sexual harmony. The group is dependent on couples' self-assessments for such issues.

Often, at this phase, initial assessment goals are reviewed to give members a clearer evaluation of the progress made. Members are sometimes astounded by how "long ago" the problems of last year seem. There is an atmosphere of sadness about ending the remarkable experience of the group, mixed with the pride and "team spirit" which come from hard work.

Resistance at this stage usually shows itself in an unwillingness to recontract for another year even though the other group members, the leaders, and perhaps even the spouse believe this is very much indicated. Members may find it quite daunting to resist such concerted forces. However, if the couple have already changed a good deal, the resisting partner may just be too frightened to go even further.

For the leaders, moving a group from beginning to end is the journey of parenthood revisited, but this time the developing youngsters are couples in a community of couples. The fruits of one's labors are very sweet when, at the end of the group, the youngsters, their marriages, and the couples community have grown to a greater level of independent functioning and life satisfaction.

7.
Designing Effective Structured Interventions

*So, you have two speeds, Off and Sledgehammer, and you want
something in between.*

—Ben to Ted

Much of the second half of each session is spent executing a specially
designed structured exercise. At the bathroom break after the unstructured
part of the group, the leaders meet and design or choose an activity which is
likely to deepen or refine the learning which was begun in the first portion of
the session. If, for example, the group has been discussing the parts of
themselves which embarrass, humiliate, or shame them, the leaders might
design an exercise on the impact of poor self-esteem in a marriage and on
careers. In this chapter, we review concepts necessary to assist leaders in
designing their own exercises.

BASIC CHOICES OF EXERCISES

How do we choose and design the exercises? They are garnered from our
knowledge of group dynamics and family therapy, from our knowledge of the
couples in therapy and from our own existential view of human intimacy in
marriage. The exercises are *not* a grab bag of things to spring on a group. As in
Strategic Family Therapy, our exercises are formulated by our thinking of the
entire group as a system and structuring a clinical intervention which is likely
to "unstick" some members or the group as a whole. There are five basic
exercise modalities, each performing a specific and useful function for the life

and growth of the group and its members. Let's look at each. Examples are found in this chapter and in Appendix B. The five modalities are:

1. Writing exercises
2. Guided imagery
3. Directed verbal sharing
4. Sociogram activities
5. Dramatic activities

1. Writing Exercises

Each group member takes paper and pencil and responds to a question. Each member or couple then write down his/her/their responses to the question posed. After sufficient time, couples share their responses with each other.

Writing tasks enable cognitive exploration of a particular issue, sharing thoughts and feelings with a partner or with the whole group. Typical topics range broadly.

Exercises of this nature can be written or drawn. Recently, we asked a beginning group to think of the marital moments which caused them the greatest pain in the last week. Then each individual was to write down his/her incident before sharing it with the partner and with the group. The writing cements the thoughts of the group member and eliminates the danger that a partner will be influenced by the response of another group member in thinking of his or her own response.

2. Guided Imagery

Here the group members are put into a relaxed state through some mild induction or muscle relaxation instructions as described by Lazarus (1971). While in the relaxed state, the group members are given an instruction to visualize a particular scene or encounter (Singer & Pope, 1978; Leuner, 1969). After allowing sufficient time for each to become involved in his/her visual adventure, the group members are gently brought back "into the room." Each person is then encouraged to share with the group some of the discoveries made while in the slightly altered state of consciousness which was somewhat closer to their unconscious processes.

Guided Imagery enables members to get in touch with preconscious feelings and beliefs about certain issues in relation to self, spouse, family of origin, children, or others.

One evening we led guided imagery concerning intimacy in marriage. Judith gave these instructions:[*]

JC: Now that your eyes are closed . . . everybody close your eyes . . . and your bodies are in a relaxed state, I want you to pay full attention to my voice as I take you on a personal adventure. What you experience will be safe and will help you to know yourself and your marriage better. Think of your marriage and of the problems that brought you to the couples group. I would like you to choose one problem which interferes with the level of intimacy you want to experience with your spouse. I want you to think for a moment now about how you feel about your problem. Think of one problem which gets in the way of intimacy with your spouse. And think about how you feel about this problem. After you have chosen your problem, and you know how you feel about it, you are commissioned to sculpt the level of intimacy of one of the couples in this group. I would like you to think now of a couple that reminds you most of your own marriage. If you were a sculptor, how might you sculpt this marriage? How would you position the partners in a relation to one another?

Will chose to sculpt Erik and Nan, the couple who reminded him most of the lack of intimacy in his marriage. He was asked what meaning it had for him.

Will: Well, it really mirrors the pattern that we have going in our relationship, ah, where one of the things I do is . . . it's not . . . the particulars are different. I get very . . . I'll come in and be very picky and very like, with the subtle anger a lot which will just cut the intimacy, whereas he is afraid to not engage his mother to substitute it but, it's a similar pattern in that it prevents the intimacy from taking place here and then Denise gets depressed and, you know, is unresponsive and . . .

Denise: I tune out.

Will: Yeah, she tunes out and just like Nan did. That's why I picked her, because she kind of does what Denise does. The particulars are different, but it's the same pattern.

3. Directed Verbal Sharing

In this simple group exercise a question is posed to the group: "How do you feel about your first name?" or "How is your relationship with your spouse

---

[*]Transcript from the videotape, *Techniques in Couples Group Therapy.*

similar to, or different from, the one with your opposite sexed parent?" Each person takes a turn at reflecting on his/her response to the question, and the group discusses the similarities between members and the meaning of the question for their marriages. Directed verbal sharing functions to help people to get to know each other, to build cohesiveness, and to foster universality or member identification with one another.

4. Sociogram Activities

A sociogram gives a group a diagram of its own internal structure. Sociograms encompass a variety of forms. In the original form as proposed by its inventor, J.L. Moreno (1951), group members are asked something on the order of, "Whom in the group would you choose as your friend if you could? You are limited to three choices." Many other forms of the sociogram have evolved. For example, the whole group may stand up and members express their choices through their body position to each other. Sociogram activities function to increase member awareness of the group structure and of each member's position in the group.

In one couples group, we used the following version of the sociogram: We distributed two kinds of tokens (in fact, we used two colors of Dixie cups). Each person received 10 each of the two kinds. The first kind was called the "influence cups." Each group member was to take his or her 10 influence tokens and give these out to the people in the group, according to how much influence they believed each person had in the group (leaders excluded, self included). Thus, one could give five to 10 tokens to a very powerful person and zero to someone who had very little power in the group.

After these tokens had been distributed, each person was asked to give out his/her ten "trust tokens" (the other color of Dixie cups). These were to be given out according to how much one trusted each individual in the group. Again, each member was allowed to give from zero to 10 cups to any given individual. After this round, each person sat there with two piles of cups, influence and trust. The difference, as usual, was quite remarkable: One person, Jack, a "feared autocrat" type, held a large number of influence tokens and very few trust tokens, while two of the women in the group had collected many trust cups and very few influence cups, a strong indication that these were people with a potential for leadership who were too afraid and too shy to use it. Other group members also received valuable feedback about how they were seen by the rest of the group.

All of the sociogram activities allow the group to get a better understanding of their own dynamics and of the perceived status of various people in the group. Sometimes, people's feelings get hurt from the exercise and their anxiety is mobilized. Most of the time, however, the activity arouses great interest and vigor in the group. It is worthwhile to tell the group that the results are only temporary, that they are bound to change, and that the member can work to change his/her role in the group. Sometimes, it is worth repeating the sociogram after a few months to let the group see how it has changed in its own internal structure and to give the group a sense of its power to change patterns which are not working well.

5. Dramatic Activities

In this group of exercises, modifications of psychodrama (Moreno & Moreno, 1959), role playing (Langley & Langley, 1983), and sculpting (Papp, 1976) are included. At times, it is worthwhile for a couple to sculpt a particular family problem (Papp, 1982). At other times a couple may role-play a particular scene which another couple had described. Sometimes, a combination of two techniques appears, despite leader instructions to the contrary.

After the instructions concerning the guided imagery about marital intimacy mentioned earlier in this chapter, Will, the man who had been sculpting, worked with the group as follows:*

JC: Okay which couple did you choose?

Will: Ah, Erik and Nan.

JC: Okay, if you like, you can include Erik's mother in your sculpture, if you believe that she is really central to their marriage.

Will: Okay, do you want me to talk about it, or just to like . . . I, I did picture her.

JC: You did picture her. Why don't you choose people to represent Erik and Nan. Just go ahead and sculpt. Do you need us to move the furniture at all?

Will: Yeah, I think we will, because I pictured it as a scene at the dining room table with Nan and Erik.

JC: Okay. Who's who?

Will: Denise will be Nan, and Nate, Nate, you'll be Erik and Dale will be Erik's mother. What I'd like you to do, um, bring your chair over here. Erik and Nan, you might want to watch really carefully. Now bring your chair into here. This is the dining room table. And, um, Nate we need you in the middle. And Nan's in the middle and mother and Erik are in. . . . Bring your chair in a little more. Nan's in the middle. What I want you to do is, I want you to . . . this is a formal, you know, formal dinner. It's not in the new kitchen, it's in the dining room, okay? It's very formal, you know, there are mirrors and you just look at this room and kind of get, you know. And, um (to Nate) you have to really be resisting talking to Nan and considering

---

*Transcript from the videotape, *Techniques in Couples Group Psychotherapy*.

her opinion. You're really looking at your mother and, um, you're not really happy, okay, but you're engaged in a conversation. (To Denise) You are having your third scotch. You are not talking. You are really depressed. I mean you are depressed. You are very, just, you're not a part of it. And can only . . . (to Dale) you're confused in a way. You're delighted to be there. You know, it's your dining room and everything, but you're not . . . you're no . . . you're not sparkling because you're dining with this couple. And you have to really be, you know, you're kind of putting up with the situation 'cause you don't really know what to do. It's not your place to really call this one. And, um, you're reluctant to. . . .You don't give her any view. You know. Okay, I want you to get into this now.

Nate: So, mother, how was the trip to the store today, the grocery store?
Dale: Oh, it was just fine. It was nice to get out. I had a good time.
Denise: That's great!
Dale: What I was wondering about was how the garden was coming in the back, whether you've worked on that section that we talked about, with the rose bushes or not.
Nate: Ah, um, not, I haven't, but I'll have the men come over and they'll be working on it next week.
Dale: I was wondering what the design looked like for that section that we talked about the other night. Because I saw these wonderful roses at the nursery near the store where I was and I just wondered what you were planning for that section.
Nate: I have some preliminary sketches. I'll be happy to show them to you.
Denise: Did you think about my idea for the garden?
Nate: Well, mother and I had already talked about what we were going to do back in that corner, so. . . .

   Occasionally the therapist may feel that a particular couple's struggle is reminiscent of some well-known couple in the literature (e.g. Romeo and Juliet, Anthony and Cleopatra, or Ginger Rogers and Fred Astaire) and may ask the group to act it out. Amidst all the hilarity that ensues, some profound learning takes place. Dramatic activities function to provide a powerful, direct, experiential learning, which can later be reflected upon via group discussion.

CONTENT OF THE EXERCISES

   Many of the exercises deal with life issues or human emotions, such as fear, anger, emotional expression which may seem unrelated to being part of a couple. Other exercises are directly linked to all couples' problems and are issues that trouble most couples. We call the latter group of these themes the "Universals of Marriage" and they affect us all. These are:

1. Sex.
2. Money.
3. In-laws and family of origin.
4. Children.
5. Illness and Death.

1. Sex

While it is natural for couples to experience temporary sexual difficulty at some time, it is the inability to communicate about sexual differences and to negotiate around those differences which produces enduring sexual difficulties. Thus, when the group decides to work on sexuality, the work centers around helping couples to talk about sexual matters and to find ways in which they can communicate their wishes and fears without antagonizing their partners.

For example, one of the exercises we use to get couples to communicate about sexual matters is to split the group for half an hour into men's and women's sections. We find that people are often more willing to initiate a discussion of sexual issues with members of their own gender than in a mixed group. In the one-gender groups, people are asked to discuss a specific question. Later they can choose to share their answers with the whole group or only with their partner. Most opt to discuss issues with the group and the "ice" has been broken for a highly self-disclosing discussion of sexuality in the lives of couples.

2. Money

We believe that since the "sexual revolution" money has replaced sex as the major couples conflict. We always look for family-of-origin issues in working with couples around financial issues. Unless there is financial hardship, money difficulties between partners usually arise because each partner came into the marriage with a set of unstated expectations and priorities for the handling of money, which turned out to be very different from the unstated expectations of the partner. Exercises in the form of writing activities or fantasized priorities about how to use money help couples to see how similar their own ideas about money often are to those of their parents. This enables the couple to understand that they are unwittingly continuing parental struggles and disagreements. This awareness alone often leads to an improvement in negotiation capacity.

Morris' Dad made money. Lots of money. He died of a heart attack at 51, when Morris was 18. Morris took over the business and believed it was his mission to make more money out of his Dad's money. When he fell in love with Leslie, he and his family requested that she convert religions and sign a prenuptial agreement. Leslie lacked money. She grew up in a family in which money got liquidated through alcoholism. When she married Morris, she was only 22 and willingly changed religions and signed the prenuptial agreement.

What Leslie didn't know, however, was that Morris equated his money with power, including power over Leslie. Nasty fights ensued about cars, houses, travel costs, clothing—various areas in which Leslie came to feel controlled and undervalued. Morris became more attacking, insulting Leslie as a "flaky" girl who was rolling in his money. When their couples group talked about the way the various couples handled money, Morris was amazed to discover that his father's way might be the downfall of both his marriage and his health, unless the couple were were able to change.

3. In-Laws and Family of Origin

One of the most important tasks facing each couple is to form a marital unit which has its own solidarity and independence, but to do so without alienating the respective families of origin of each partner. Simplistic or drastic solutions (e.g. cutting off ties) cause considerable grief in the future of the couple. Continued dependence on parents or siblings robs the couple of its own identity. There is little choice but to individuate. Bringing this conflict into the open, where couples can try to process it, can be freeing for many group members.

Dealing with the aging parent(s) of either partner is a subcategory in the in-laws group of issues. The parents' dependence on the younger couple creates new challenges which may overwhelm the strength of the couple. The death of a parent and the emotional turmoil created by this event strain the marriage further.

4. Children

In the "good old days," couples married and had babies. No longer. The choice of whether or not to have children and at what point in the development of the marriage is a task which represents a major hurdle for many couples. Once the choice has been made and children are there, differing expectations of who-is-responsible-for-what produce marital dilemmas. As the children get older, issues of triangulation and playing parents against each other become new tests of marital strength. When one is designing an exercise for couples around children, it is frequently difficult to find something that touches each couple in the group. Most of the time, the group members are at different developmental stages as far as the raising of children is concerned. Only more broad-based difficulties, such as the amount of time allotted for career vs. children vs. spouse, touch all couples, with or without children.

One of the most powerful exercises is deceptively simple. Each person in the group ranks the importance of three issues: financial stability, children, marriage. No ties are allowed and ranking must be done quickly. After each has written down his/her ranking, partners take turns in reading out their hierarchy. The discrepancies between two marriage partners are usually quite remarkable and present an excellent stimulus for discussion. It is important in the discussion to clarify that no superiority of one answer over the other is implied in the question, but that differences in rankings may be giving a couple trouble and are deserving of further attention.

One night, as we were doing this exercise, Ellis came up with a ranking of (1) financial stability, (2) children, (3) marriage, while his wife, Jaime, chose (1) children, (2) marriage, and (3) financial stability. In the discussion, Ellis at first maintained that by placing such high priority on the financial security for his family he was, in fact, doing what was best for his family and deserved praise for it. Jaime expressed sadness and concern that for Ellis the children were only second and the marriage third. The recognition of this shocked the couple into exploring their fear of intimacy in the marriage by being so involved in career and raising of children.

It turned out that attendance in the group was the *only* activity the couple were doing together without the involvement of the children. It was this discovery that prompted Ellis and Jaime to decide to pay more attention to their marriage outside of the group, to set more time aside to be with each other, and to explore the substantial blocks to marital intimacy.

5. Illness and Death

At some point, couples also must come to grips with their own vulnerability as human beings. The physical illness of one of the partners, coming face to face with death through illness, a serious accident, or even a near miss places a new set of questions and fears before the couple. Many couples come through such a crisis with a renewed appreciation of one another. Others come through it with considerable disappointment and resentment, feeling that the other did not behave in a way which the sick partner had hoped for. If one of the couples in a group is struggling with this issue, an exercise regarding a partner's illness can be very fruitful.

As becomes clear from the above examples, the "universals of marriage" are not seen just as trouble spots and difficulties. They constitute developmental tasks which each couple need to master at some point in their development. Frequently, couples who seek help, do so because they have run into a snag with one or more of these tasks. The solutions they found had backfired and caused palpable emotional pain. Working through these problems in a caring and respectful community of others who are struggling with similar issues often opens completely new vistas for the couples and gives rise to solutions that neither of the partners and neither of the leaders could have thought of alone.

SEVEN STEPS IN DEVELOPING A GROUP EXERCISE

In our workshops on couples group psychotherapy, numerous colleagues have asked us *how* to design original group exercises. To facilitate learning, we have broken the exercise process into a seven step procedure, which is further elaborated below.

1. Check the climate of the group.
2. Choose a theme for the exercise.
3. Take a leader's time out while the group takes a break.
4. Design the exercise spontaneously.
5. Execute the exercise in the group.
6. Process the exercise with the group.
7. Record the exercise for future use.

1. Check the Climate of the Group

Groups have climates just like any other environment. Groups can be hot and dry, hot and steamy, cool and damp, frosty, bright and sunny. Group leaders can see thunder clouds approaching in a group and can see the sun breaking through the clouds of an early part of a session. The metaphor is useful for leaders and can be taught to members, who can use it as part of their group work. In the first part of each group meeting, we do a climate check with or without involving members in the discussion. This enables us to work with the level of affect in the group and to intensify or charge it through work with the group as a whole and by structuring exercises which keep the existing climate of the group in mind.

Considering the climate in the group is as important as responding to the topic. One does not, for example, take a joyous group and lead it in an exercise on death, unless the joy is actually denial of an upsetting rumble in the group. It is necessary to assess the mood of the whole group before designing an exercise and to keep in mind the developmental stage of the group and how people are coping with it.

2. Choose a Theme for the Exercise

To choose a fitting theme, it is necessary to listen to the issues which the group has been actively working on or avoiding. Exercises can then be experienced by the group either like a requested dance or like a surprise. In the latter case, members may feel as if they were caught. In the former, the feeling is more like, "They are playing our song." Whichever it may be, the group ultimately needs to see the usefulness of the choice lest it feel uncomfortable and out of place.

It is also important for the leaders to take the risk of using the exercise to confront a cohesive group with issues it has been avoiding. Not all exercises will turn into rousing successes and one has to be willing to risk an occasional mistake in the choice of the theme, the type of exercise, or its timing.

> One group was ready to tape, except for Ted, a member with exceptionally low self-esteem and a negative distortion of his perception of his appearance. A number of other group members were also involved in the self-esteem theme. We encouraged Ted to allow the taping, which he did. Then we designed a structured exercise for the taping which centered on the themes of valuing of self in relation to self, spouse, and peers. Not only did Ted and the other members get to continue working on the theme, but they could intensify their own learning by adding the visual component of the taping. In this way, avoidance by the group of the taping by electing Ted to turn it down turned into a direct confrontation of the resistance by the choice of the structured exercise.

3. Take a Leaders' Time Out While the Group Takes a Break

Before making the choice of theme and designing the procedure, the leaders need to separate physically from the group. This can be during the break or in the time period between sessions. Trying to design an exercise while also trying to conduct a group is distracting and drains the leaders' energies away from the group.

During the break between the unstructured and structured sections, the leaders can think about the theme, the mood in the group, and the energy level of the group. For example, if the group appears slow and tired, one may want to think of a very lively activity which is likely to reactivate people.

4. Design the Exercise Spontaneously

This is the point of the creative leap. After taking the necessary information into account, the leaders need to let their imaginations run free and come up with an activity which will stimulate the group to work on the issue at hand. Sometimes, a procedure like "brainstorming" can help: Leaders allow themselves to come up with zany, outlandish ideas at first and then figure out how they can be shaped in such a way that they perform the task without losing too much of their spunk or seeming absurd to the group.

Creating a group exercise is analogous to inventing the homework assignments which are given by strategic family therapists. An activity is being set up which enables "listening by doing," but in a group this is done for the whole group instead of for one couple or family. The task can be straightforward or paradoxical. Whatever it turns out to be, a well-designed structured exercise is an invitation to people to engage in an activity which will shift their reality frame on the particular issue which is being worked on.

No one can expect the group leaders to be creative on every group night. There are times when it is perfectly reasonable to fall back on a "canned" exercise — a structure suggested in the literature. The works by Pfeiffer and Jones (1974) and Satir (1988) give a wealth of practical activities which can be used with or without modification in a session. There are some advantages to using preexisting exercises. For example, when the group is coping with a typical developmental issue, it is useful to utilize an exercise which has been shown to bring this stage into focus.

One activity we like to use in the first or second session is a type of directed verbal sharing in which we ask each couple to share with the group how they met. Or we ask: "Tell the group what you found attractive about your partner when you first met." This exercise is a metaphor for getting to know people and for making oneself known. It also helps the members to introduce themselves and their partners in a positive manner. We often say that a new group is a bit like a group "blind date," and we enable the metaphor to work on the group on a variety of levels.

Using a "canned" exercise cuts down on the stress on the leaders. It is very difficult to be creative when there is time pressure. It is also quite difficult to be creative session after session, especially if one is not feeling well or if there is tension in the co-leader relationship.

Naturally, in using a "canned" exercise, there is the danger that it will be listless. Like a prepackaged macaroni and cheese dinner in a cardboard box, the flavor might be lost. But often it is not necessary to come up with a whole new recipe each time; often it is quite legitimate to take a quick look at one's recipe file and add a bit of flavor or modify the dish slightly to fit the tastes of the diners.

To summarize, the exercise can be verbal or nonverbal. It uses whatever skills the clinician has available. Part of the creativity is making the fullest use of the leaders' skill, training, and expertise. Thus, the exercise might involve psychodrama (or at least psychodramatic techniques), sculpting, guided imagery, active listening, genograms, reminiscences, and life-altering decisions. A vibrant co-therapy team, like a vibrant marital couple, can thoroughly enjoy the lively and creative teamwork which helps give birth to the exercise.

5. Execute the Exercise in the Group

As the group reconvenes after the break, there is often an expectant mood — members wait for a cue from the leaders about what is "in store for them" for the balance of the session. They quickly become accustomed to trusting the judgment of the leaders, if past exercises have been successful and rich. Like the audience waiting for the play to start, they allow themselves to become alive and reactive to the instructions by the leaders. The group becomes a kind of "class" of students, eager to experience the multilevel stimulations from "teachers" they have come to enjoy and to trust. The foundation of the trust enables them to free their own spontaneity and creativity, and the richness of the tapestry of leaders and members becomes assembled as the multilevel experience unfolds. For here, unlike in the theater, *they* are the actors and the audience in their very own production.

6. Process the Exercise with the Group

Members need to put their experiential learning into a perspective which incorporates the new information into previous learning. Processing the experience through discussion enables this incorporation to occur.

The processing also gives the leaders a glimpse of the learning that the members actually received. One may be in for a surprise and the conclusions drawn may be very different from the ones which had been intended or expected when the exercise was designed. More often the learning received is only slightly different but leaves room for the leader to add perspective or make some other kind of adjustment.

7. Record the Exercise for the Future

Making notes of the exercise used gives the leaders a record of the activities in the group and the learning that took place. It also offers the possibility of using the information later in the group as an illustration of certain points, or of using the exercise in another group.

After a group had done the Noah's Ark exercise and Jack had presented himself and his wife as a pair of otters, stressing the lifelong mutual dependency these animals have on each other, the theme of dependency in the couple became central in subsequent sessions. Returning to the metaphor of the otters, members and leaders could make a point in a more acceptable and humorous way than by using direct confrontation.

THE ANXIETY OF SPONTANEITY

These exercises are somewhat like a chemistry experiment in school. The experiment does not always work, sometimes it falls flat, or the point it was supposed to make was not made. Yet, it is important that leaders be willing to take the risk of having an exercise backfire or fizzle out. It is only this kind of risk taking which allows the group to grow, keeps the leaders alive, and gives the members courage to try new behaviors. The exercises require a sense of humor on the part of everyone, especially the members. Frequently an exercise may seem silly or funny at first, and the important message or shock of recognition comes only after everyone has participated in good spirits.

People must become vulnerable enough to each other to create a working bond. The vibrancy of the group will be the reward for doing so. For the therapists, too, a vibrant, hardworking group is the reward for the challenge presented by having to design an activity which responds to the turmoil and learning needs of a particular group with a multitude of couples issues at a specific moment in its development.

PART III

Integrating Theory, Research, and Treatment for Couples in Groups

8.

The Intervention Hierarchy: Four Levels

If I were to give the group a symbolic gift, it would be a bridge . . .
we would all be on different sides of a large terrain and we
would meet on the bridge.

— Ted

A visitor observing a couples group in action will find the group absorbed in some kind of subject matter. The content of the group's work ranges from the trivial to the most profound and from pre-group social banter to an intense grappling with life-threatening issues. In our couples group, for example, issues on a given evening can range from the quality of the mustard at the gourmet shop where clients buy coffee before the group meets to a member's prognosis after a heart attack.

It is only logical, then, that an observer would wonder how we decide when to intervene, when not to intervene, and how to intervene. Further, an observer would question whether one type of intervention is preferable to another and, if so, how a leader chooses one type of intervention over another. These questions are crucial to the welfare of the group, and to the quality of the treatment. The types of interventions available to the leaders of couples group therapy are varied and rich. The issues around therapeutic interventions deserve a great deal of consideration. Many of our interventions depend on our own maps as therapists.

The logic behind our interventions is best understood through the metaphor of the "therapist's map." Imagine, for a moment, trying to drive from New York to Kansas without a decent map. You have some notion that Kansas is west of Kentucky. Last time you went to Kansas, you flew, and have no idea of which roads intersect with which highways, how much in tolls and gas is required, or how much time to estimate for travel. All you know is that it is west of Kentucky, and it is far. What would you pay for a decent map before starting your journey? Plenty.

A therapist's map, as the term implies, refers to a tool in the mind of the therapist. It is a cognitive written or unwritten organizational framework, understood by the therapist, which includes components necessary for engineering the treatment. In individual therapy, a therapist's map includes a working understanding of the diagnostic essentials and treatment strategies for a client or client system. When the client system is a couple, the therapist's map must also include the structure of the couple's relationship along typical interactive dimensions, along with an understanding of the intergenerational issues for each partner.

When the client system is a couples psychotherapy group, still another dimension is crucial: a group map of the subgroups and dyads, and an understanding of the properties of the group as a whole (such as norms, roles, cohesiveness, and leadership patterns) in the various stages of the group's development over time. Naturally, the therapist's map of a couples psychotherapy group is complex, and can best be charted through an understanding of couples/family therapy and of group therapy.

Organizing the content of a group's activity efficiently and sensibly has been discussed frequently in the theoretical and research literature in group psychotherapy (Flapan, 1981). Borriello (1979) directs his attention to the leader in proposing an organizational map which highlights three "intervention foci": the personal, the interpersonal, and the group-as-a-whole. Each forms a level for therapeutic intervention. In our opinion, an added dimension is present in couples psychotherapy groups.

THE INTERVENTION CHOICES

In order to include the richness and complexity of the couples dimension in our organizational scheme for couples group psychotherapy, we must expand Borriello's (1979) concept in two ways. The first includes the ability of the leader to intervene at the level of marital interaction itself. This is couples psychotherapy in a group setting. Thus, the therapist has an additional possible focus, viz, the dynamics between two partners. The second expansion has more sweeping ramifications for the group and for the therapists. We find it useful to consider that the intervention foci choices can be made not only by the leaders, as Borriello suggests, but also by the group members themselves who can direct their attention spontaneously to these foci in the course of group work. Thus, we refer to these foci as levels of intervention or as levels of interaction.

Let us consider in more detail this proposed four-way classification of group content. According to this scheme, the activity of a group can take place on any one of these four levels at any time, as well as on a combination of more than one level simultaneously. These levels of intervention are:

1. Personal level, in which group talk is centered on one individual.
2. Couples level, in which the group focuses on one of the couples.
3. Interpersonal level, in which interpersonal relationships between two or more members or couples are in focus. If the group's attention is on two people, these are not intimate partners, but rather members of a subgroup, or cross-couple interaction.
4. Group-as-a-whole level, in which the group works on its own group process.

1. Personal Level

At this level, group members work intensively with an individual group member. At times this looks like individual therapy in the presence of others, but there are moments at which this is the intervention of choice in order to make possible the most powerful impact on a person.

Todd had been an active and central member of the group for quite a while. His comments were thoughtful, emphatic, and extremely helpful to other group members. Yet, over the last few months he had become increasingly withdrawn and silent. After two or three such sessions the group members became alarmed by Todd's atypical behavior. When they directed their attention to him, it became clear that through a very unsettling incident at work, Todd had become preoccupied with his presumed inability to control his anger, which sometimes pushed him to lash out at others at work and which could cost him his job. From there he had gone into an obsessive worrying about his personality and the future economic well-being of his young family. Working intensively with Todd in the group (using a combination of cognitive approaches and family-of-origin material), the group helped Todd to overcome his obsession and regain his pivotal position in the group.

2. Couples Level

A group working in the couples mode may spend time on the dynamics of one particular couple.

Lee and Nate had spent the previous Saturday afternoon embroiled in one of their usual pre-dinner-party fights. The group knew the fights well: Lee accuses Nate of not helping enough. Nate accuses Lee of being too anxious in her need to set a perfect table and of ordering him around. On this particular Saturday, Lee had decided that the dinner party needed an additional, complex chocolate "gateau" and had quietly escaped from their agreed-upon joint garden work to go to the store to buy a special type of baking chocolate. When she returned, Nate blew his stack, withdrew, and refused to help at all. By the time the guests arrived, they found a perfectly set table, a chocolate gateau baked to perfection, and enough tension between host and hostess to produce indigestion.

After hearing this report, the group moved in to work with them. Both Lee and Nate were confronted with the ineffectiveness of their style of conflict resolution and were given alternate methods to try the "next time." One group member told Lee that her house was, in fact, too perfect for guests to feel at home. She asked Lee to leave a few details undone. Lee agreed to try, but thought the assignment was very tough. Nate was encouraged to stay and discuss issues as best he could, rather than to explode and withdraw.

The group also worked directly with the communication style employed by Lee and Nate. They told Lee she talked too quickly, barraging Nate with her flow of words. They helped Nate to talk more directly with Lee in the group, where he felt safer than at home. In the course of the year, the group helped Lee and Nate to communicate more effectively with one another.

3. Interpersonal Level

The activity of the group is often focused on interpersonal relationships between members or couples in the group. Members learn that others are struggling with similar issues and discover that they can be helpful to each other by sharing similar struggles and their attempted solutions. Many of Yalom's (1975) "curative factors," such as universality and altruism, can come to full bloom in this mode of working. At times, the mere discovery of similarities is healing, at other times only a more extensive sharing of experiences can bring about therapeutic change.

Three of the four couples present one evening were having major conflicts with gender roles. All three husbands were self-employed and quite successful, while their wives tended to home and children. All three couples had entered their marriages with the unstated marital contract that earning a living and making major decisions was the responsibility of the man of the house. The men said, in effect, "I'm earning the money so *I* decide how it is to be spent or invested." They considered it their inalienable right to make major (and some minor) family decisions (vacations, business moves, social engagements). While this understanding was unquestioned at the time of marriage, increasing maturation and changing attitudes in our society had moved the women to become progressively more dissatisfied. One had developed a quiet but powerful stance of passive resistance which made it impossible for the husband to carry out many of his plans; the other two had resorted to arguing vociferously, which was equally as paralyzing. All three women isolated their husbands from major decisions regarding "their" children. In all three couples the result was persistent marital frustration; no one was getting his/her needs met. Decisions were often made by inaction and the general interactive stance was one of being stuck in concrete.

The group soon discovered the similarities among them. At first, the women supported each other to fight for greater marital decision-making power, whereupon the men insulted the women and threw up their collective hands in disgust and frustration. The fourth couple joined in by proposing solutions which had worked well for their marriage. Going over this theme and using a variety of examples and exercises, the couples were able to find different ways of decision making. As sessions progressed, assertiveness replaced bickering and outright disagreements replaced passive aggressiveness. Men and women learned to ask directly for what they needed and to attempt to work out discrepancies between needs cooperatively.

4. Group-as-a-Whole Level

The group, with or without help from the leader, takes on a group issue. Directional shifts, group decisions, norm enforcement, or explorations of participants' roles in the group are all topics of discussion which fall into the group-as-a-whole category. In order to be successful, the group has to work out problems in its own dynamics. Lewin (1951) provided seminal thinking on the centrality of context. Some of these problems are part of the natural development of groups described elsewhere (Schein & Bennis, 1965; Thelen, 1954; MacKenzie & Livesley, 1983). Themes like developing a mature relationship with the leader, with minimal dependence or counterdependence, fall into this category.

Other problems may not be common to all groups but are unique and stem from the particular constellation of people in the room. For example, a monopolizer can drain group energies, while an acerbic relationship between two members can prevent the group from working independently. Group-as-a-whole work enables the group to progress developmentally from dependence through cohesiveness to interdependence. Without this intervention level, a group is in danger of remaining stuck in an early developmental stage. While it is possible to gain therapeutic benefits in such a group, the results are likely to be less substantial than in a group which has gained some mastery over its group dynamics and is better able to control its own destiny.

> One of our groups was stuck for some time in a mode in which one couple, Morris and Leslie, came in session after session to work on some variation of a continuing fight which often sounded superficial to the other group members. Despite a desire to be helpful to this couple, the group began to show a general sense of annoyance with Morris and Leslie and impatience with their trials. When two other group members, Brad and Connie, finally expressed their dissatisfaction with the group's work, the group moved to a stage in which greater honesty, risk taking, and confrontation were required in order to keep growing. Morris and Leslie had merely acted on behalf of those in the group who were afraid to go on to the next, more frightening level of interaction.
>
> Dealing with the superficiality of the interaction between Morris and Leslie brought into the open the group's resistance to moving on and served as a metaphor for the superficiality in the group. It enabled the group to work out the conflict and reassured the more anxious members so that more meaningful work became possible. Brad and Connie benefitted by the leadership they showed in the group, while Morris and Leslie were forced to encounter each other more honestly. Thus, the work of one couple acted as a metaphor, enabling interventions regarding the group as a whole.

Improving group functioning by working at a group-as-a-whole level is of central importance (Agazarian & Peters, 1981). Obviously, it is never stated as the therapeutic goal by members entering a couples group. People enter group therapy because they need change at the individual or couple level. They care about the proper functioning of the group and about understanding its mechanisms only insofar as it helps them to gain from the process therapeutically. For most members, working out group process issues is only a means to an end, albeit a very significant one. Successful mastery of a troublesome group problem is nearly always viewed as a significant therapeutic step for the group.

While we do believe that there is a group atmosphere which is observable and open to influence by the leaders, individual members, or subgroupings, we want to discourage mythologizing the concept. The whole group is a gestalt, i.e. a configuration having more power than the members taken singly, a system greater than the sum of its parts. However, a concept of a "group mind" can encourage vague and mystical interventions. In fact, many directional shifts in a group are not made by the group as a whole, but instead by a few influential members (or even just one), with the rest of the group remaining silently attentive and eventually following suit.

MEMBERS ASSUME LEADERSHIP

Many shifts in the level of group interaction occur not because the therapist chooses the shift but because the group so chooses. A couple may raise a topic on the couple's level of interaction by introducing a particular marital conflict. Soon, other members chime in, discussing similar problems in their marriages, and members move the group activity to an interpersonal level. Such shifts may occur several times in the course of any session and feel natural and comfortable to everyone involved. When this occurs spontaneously, there is no necessity for the leaders to intervene in this process of shifting levels. The group is doing its work unaided. However, the leaders do need to remain aware of the change of levels and must determine whether this shift might be a sign of group avoidance and of trouble.

> One night, Jane became very critical of the female group therapist, accusing her of being unethical, unprofessional, and not helpful. Both therapists tried to help her to understand their interpretation of the difficulty, but Jane was alternately attacking and silently morose. Group members kept changing the topic of discussion from this highly charged interpersonal level of interaction between a female client and her female therapist to safer topics like couple arguments and personal problems.
>
> Finally, the group leaders chose to move onto the group-as-a-whole level and made an interpretation to the group that Jane's anger was also a group issue and that Jane was speaking for the group in expressing her anger over the female therapist's upcoming two-session absence (due to teaching obligations). In this case, allowing members to control shifts in level of interaction would have kept the group stuck in anger, discomfort, and avoidance. It also might have resulted, later, in scapegoating against Jane or in Jane's need to withdraw from her investment in the group, in order to try to handle her anger.

MIXING INTERACTIVE LEVELS

On some occasions, it may be difficult to detect the level of group interaction. Work on two levels can go on simultaneously. For example, one group member may focus intensively on family-of-origin conflicts, while another couple is working out something critical to their own marriage by helping the person who is working on the family-of-origin material. Thus, while the one member is working on an individual level, the two others are working on a couples level.

> After months of avoidance, Nan gathered her courage and told the couples group that she drank too much. She described sipping scotch while preparing dinner as a way to ease the emptiness and loneliness she experienced in her marriage. During her painful confession, Erik, Nan's husband, was equally involved in the discussion. Dale took the role of the "respectful inquirer," gently encouraging Nan and Erik to explore the marital issues in more depth. Dale's contribution was extremely helpful to Nan and Erik, and an observer would have seen Dale working at the couples level of interaction. However, Dale was simultaneously dealing with her own painful years spent as the child of an alcoholic mother.

This simultaneity of levels is actually quite rare. More often, leaders can sit back and listen to the group work on one level, then another, then back to the first, and on to a third, and so on. It is a bit like sitting at the ballet during a performance of Tchaikovsky's Nutcracker at Christmastime. First one gets the gestalt of all the children in the party scene. Then one concentrates only on Fritz, the impish brother who breaks the nutcracker. Then one watches Fritz with Marie, his sister. And finally, one watches only the lovely little girls rocking their dolls in the center of the stage as the adults cluster around them. All levels of activity are, in fact, going on simultaneously, but one level after another becomes the focal point of the drama which unfolds on the stage and captivates the attention of the viewer.

THE FLUIDITY OF A GROUP IN PROGRESS

A shifting of levels is often a useful and natural occurrence in a couples group. It indicates that the group is ready to move to a different subject or is ready to expand the subject at hand. The group may need to include more people to make things more interesting or to work more intensely by focusing on fewer members. However, a shifting of levels can also be a sign of a group in trouble. Sometimes groups spend so much time moving about between these levels of interaction that one gets the feeling of aimless chaos and lack of focus. Frequently, this phenomenon does not even appear as a shift from one level to another. Instead, a group discussion takes place at one level while it becomes clear that the matter should be worked on at a different level. It is reminiscent of the scene in Crane's *The Red Badge of Courage* where the soldier has held his battle position valiantly with great fear and turmoil, only to be told later that the real battle was on another hill.

The therapist or a member may observe or decide that the group is misdirecting its energies. For example, a group works ad nauseam at a couples level when there is a burning group issue lying dormant. When a therapist or group member becomes aware that avoidance is occurring, it is essential that group energies be refocused.

FOUR TYPES OF MISDIRECTED GROUP ENERGIES

Despite all good intentions, groups get confused, anxious, and out of synch. Following are four instances in which this can happen and create larger problems if not checked:

1. Split ambivalence.
2. Fighting a couple's problem with someone else's partner.
3. Fighting a group problem as an interpersonal problem.
4. Couples fights as diversions.

1. Split Ambivalence

In this marital pattern an *internal* conflict present in each partner is played out as a *marital* argument. In actuality, each partner is highly ambivalent about the issue in conflict, but each projects one side of the ambivalence onto the other partner, keeping the other side for him/herself.

Wolfgang and Lisl, an immigrant couple nearing retirement age, had repeated arguments about whether to return to their homeland or to stay in the Untied States. Most times it was Wolfgang who wanted to return to "the old country" and Lisl who wanted to stay, but sometimes the two shifted positions, having the same argument with their roles exchanged. The points raised were always the same: Wanting to spend one's retirement years with one's siblings and school friends conflicted with wanting to remain near one's children, grandchildren, and friends from adult life. Only after Wolfgang and Lisl were able to see that each had the same *internal* conflict were they were able to work out solutions and stop the fighting. Thus, shifting the conflict from the personal to a couples level was what had kept them stuck; returning it to an individual level proved helpful.

2. Fighting Out a Couple's Problem With Someone Else's Partner

This happens frequently when a marriage partner is getting internally ready to tackle a problem in the marriage, but as yet lacks the courage to deal with it directly. The member tries it on a person with similar personality traits.

One evening, Penny lashed out rather heatedly at another group member, Morris, for expressing his enjoyment of fast food hamburgers. Penny gave Morris a lecture on how he endangered his health by ingesting so much fat, cholesterol, sodium, and other evil substances. The group was somewhat stunned by the vehemence of Penny's lecture. Soon, however, it became clear to everyone that Penny was undergoing a deep personal crisis due to her husband Leo's recent (nonfatal) heart attack which she blamed on Leo's unhealthy affection for junk food.

3. Fighting Out a Group-as-a-Whole Problem as an Interpersonal Problem

Here, one individual takes on a particular crusade, seeming to embark on a personal battle with someone in the group. In reality, an acute group issue is being worked on.

Danielle, a relatively new client, agreed to join the group and to abide by its rules. Soon after the first few sessions, however, she began to be very critical and indignant. She especially fumed about having to pay in advance for services not received yet (members in our couples groups pay at the beginning of the month for that month's sessions). At first this seemed to be her personal issue with the leaders, but the group members' opinions on the matter were confusing and counterproductive. The discussion remained fruitless until it became clear that Danielle, in fact, was merely a spokesperson for the group which indeed was having issues with the leaders over trust. The trust issue was being expressed in terms of how money and services were to be handled. Trust for the leaders was the developmental task the group had to master in order to move on. As long as people believed that Danielle was merely fighting her own little battle, not much could be done to move the group forward.

4. Having a Couples Fight to Keep the Group From Working

This version of shifting attentional levels was discussed a few pages back and illustrated with the case of Morris and Leslie who kept the group at a lower level of functioning than it was capable of until the pattern was disrupted by two group members who became impatient with it.

It is the task of the leader to be alert and to watch for the shifts in levels. Missing their significance can cost valuable group time and keep the group stuck. Conversely, if a group is stuck for a while, it behooves the leader to search for possible manifestations of the misdirections described here. One might ask oneself: What is going on here? What could be the real issue? We suggest looking first for the group-as-a-whole as the seat of the real issue, then looking farther as needed.

THE PRINCIPLE OF ISOMORPHISM

Isomorphism is a concept well known to systems theorists. It asserts that similar structures and processes occur on several levels in related systems. Accordingly a troublesome issue can manifest itself — with some variations — on an individual level (i.e. within a member of a couple), on a couples level (between members of a couple), and on a group level (for each group member).

Amy and Paul have had a long-standing struggle over responsibility versus having fun. Amy usually takes the role of the responsible one, insisting that they work on their house on weekends instead of going boating. Paul makes sure that life for these two is not all work and no play, pushing for vacations and trips to the movies. One night in the group they were fighting about whether to spend their vacation time and their money on a trip South or to stay home and concentrate on the renovation of their house. In the group discussion it became clear that they were really struggling with a split ambivalence: Both Amy and Paul wanted to have a vacation *and* make home improvements, yet neither could choose between the two options.

From the group's rather spirited response, a matching issue on the group level became apparent: In the initial early sessions so far, the group had been working on a relatively superficial level. Members had gotten to know each other through much lighthearted banter. Now they were ready to move on to more serious therapy matters. Amy and Paul's issue became a model for the group in working out its own conflict over fun versus responsibility. It touched people on personal, couple, and group levels.

The principle of isomorphism is nothing mysterious. Understanding it and applying it to a group enables the therapist to think on several levels simultaneously, to respond with more flexibility to the challenges of the group, and to unravel otherwise strange shifts in levels.

Sympathetic Vibrations

From the foregoing discussion it becomes clear that it is to the advantage of the couples group therapist to be attuned to all four levels simultaneously. Most issues raised by a couple or individual resonate on other levels. In the world of music, a piano, when its pedal is depressed, will resonate in the appropriate string when another instrument produces that tone. In a group, other members will be affected by the struggles of an individual. Yet, as in the piano metaphor, members have to be open to the experience and the conflict has to touch a part for which they have a corresponding structure.

Awareness of the various ways in which problems manifest themselves gives the therapist a great deal of latitude in making choices. Assessing the most efficient place for intervention greatly enhances the therapist's effectiveness. There are many instances in which an intervention can be made on more than one level. Let us illustrate with Nell and Skip.

Nell opened the session with a report on her latest difficulty with her husband, Skip. She had berated him for something, he got angry, and left the house to stay at their country home for a "cooling off" period of a few days.

Because of the particular stage that the group was on, this issue could at that time be conceptualized on all four levels:

1. (*Personal*) Nell had a serious problem in curtailing her need to shape Skip's behavior through criticism. She had a long history of trying to change Skip through what she once termed "gentle browbeating." Most of the time she was, in fact, rather successful with it and got Skip to do what she wanted him to do. Occasionally, however, Skip would get very angry and leave for a few days to get away from the nagging. Only at these times did Nell become aware of the tremendous cost of her style of influence.

Skip, on the other hand, was extremely susceptible to guilt and highly vulnerable to criticism. He was an easy mark for Nell's version of behavior shaping. After a while, however, his anger would mount to a level which was frightening to him. Unable to express it in a more appropriate way, he had to resort to flight, which usually resulted in a separation of a few days. Thus, he isolated himself from his own anger.

2. (*Couple level*) Both partners were involved in a repetitive, interactive sequence in which the untoward behaviors of one partner fed those of the other. Both were profoundly unhappy with this sequence and

suffered considerably during the separations, but they were afraid to give up the pattern, afraid of change. At this stage in treatment, they distrusted each other too much to do otherwise.

3. (*Interpersonal level*) Lena and Jared, two other members in this group, had a similar issue. However, the mutual reinforcement of their behaviors was more obvious: Lena used to berate Jared for all the time he spent at work. Being new to his accounting firm, Jared felt compelled to put in extra hours in order to please his superiors. Lena resented the many hours he spent away from home and from her. She became anxious and upset when he was away. Jared would react to her complaining with considerable guilt and anger. And, to make matters worse, he would withdraw; part of his motivation to work such long hours was to be away from her.

4. (*Group-as-a-Whole level*) Expressing one's anger instead of running away was also a general issue in this group. The members were feeling some anger at one another, but were reluctant to express it. Though there was no actual staying away from the group, members felt a lessening of the desire to be there. The group was at a point of considerable opportunity. If it could work out the anger issue, greater intimacy and self-disclosure would result. However, if the members ran away emotionally, the group would remain stuck in a problem-solving mode. And though problem solving has a place in good group work, it was less than this group was capable of.

As this illustration shows, a group leader is faced with a number of options regarding the level at which one can choose to intervene. Which level is selected depends on a number of factors. However, choices need to be made with forethought and with an eye on the current status of the group and its members. There is little wisdom in merely doing what feels right or in getting caught up in the confusion of an unfocused group.

THE CHOICE OF INTERVENTION LEVELS: THERAPIST GUIDELINES

Knowledge of and sensitivity to the processes on all four interactive levels can be bewildering and may leave the therapist with the need for some handy rule of thumb which could indicate which level is the most advantageous at a given time. Unfortunately, there are no such easy rules. The decision about intervention levels needs to be made over and over in response to the changing dynamics of the group. A few general guidelines, however, are shown below:

1. There is latitude in the choice of levels.
2. Shifting levels often resolves issues.
3. Work at the level of greatest group pain.
4. Consider all levels in each group session.
5. The greater the member involvement, the better.

Let us now consider each guideline in some detail.

Guideline 1: There is Latitude in the Choice of Levels

Since there is some latitude in the choice of intervention level, selecting an ineffective level is not a major problem. At worst, it may result in boredom or flight behavior in the group. Usually, it soon becomes apparent to a therapist that a wrong tack has been taken and the members are losing interest. A skillful shifting of levels at that point can usually set things straight. Only a prolonged time span at an ineffective interactive level which fails to involve a sufficient number of members is likely to have detrimental effects.

Guideline 2: Shifting Levels Often Resolves Issues

Despite the latitude in intervention options, a shift in levels often helps in resolving an issue. If an intervention has failed on one level, one may try to attack the problem on a different level.

Jack was true to form in being verbally domineering in the group in very much the same way in which he dominated his wife, Deidre, at home. The group leaders were not very successful trying to effect a change by dealing with this problem at a couples level. After a few sessions, however, a few members in the group became annoyed with Jack's verbal style and "took him on." At this, the interpersonal level, Jack was better able to see how costly his behavior was in the long run and that more listening and less talking would be to his and to the group's advantage.

Guideline 3. Work at the Level of the Greatest Group Pain in a Cohesive Group

There is some wisdom in working at the level at which there is the most pain and the most despair. Whether one follows Freud, who insists that there must be "Leidensdruck" (pressure of suffering) in order for treatment to be successful, or Whitaker, who speaks of heightening the level of despair in order to effect change, the message is the same: On the whole, people are most amenable to change when they are in the most discomfort. The reverse of this guideline is also true: Working at a level which misses the pain and despair will feel strange or insulting to the member who is feeling it. It will also miss a valuable opportunity.

There are, however, some limitations to this guideline. The person complaining the loudest is not necessarily the one in the most pain or the one most ready to make changes. Much to the contrary, for the noisy complainer may very well enjoy the attention and care from the group but remain settled in his/her self-defeating ways. Often, it takes some astute observation by the leader or a group member to look through this pattern of complaint and no-change and stop it.

Guideline 4: Consider All Levels in Each Group Session

Over the course of a group, all levels need to be kept in mind to an adequate extent. Any prolonged neglect of one of the four levels is likely to keep the group from being as successful as it could be. Such neglect could even have a detrimental effect on the group or its members. It's very much like a family. Though the parents may focus their attention temporarily on their marriage or on one of the children, any prolonged neglect of anyone will be very troublesome. Despite the attention to all levels, sessions usually take on a tone of being mostly focused in one particular area. The research study described later in this chapter is based on the assumption of such naturally occurring imbalances.

Guideline 5: The Greater the Member Involvement the Better

Most of the time, the more members involved, actively or silently, in a discussion, the better for the group. A whole-group level of intervention, if done skillfully, can keep everyone in the group emotionally involved and working hard. In contrast, individual work can tempt people to drop out emotionally with internal self-statements like: "That's not my problem" or "This lady is weird. I'm glad I'm not like that" or "Let the leader handle it. I'll relax."

Yet there is a limitation to this rule too. There are times when intensive individual work can be inspirational to others. All these guidelines are meant only as general directives. They are in no way arbitrary and cannot replace the therapeutic acumen of the leader. Interpersonal sensitivity, experience in working with couples and groups, and a consistently high level of attention to the many simultaneous processes in the group will guide the leader to make useful intervention choices.

AN EXPERIMENTAL STUDY OF THE INTERVENTION LEVELS

Goals and Objectives

Although interventions are usually brief and momentary events and the levels can shift a great deal during a session, a given group session usually takes on an atmosphere of being focused more on one level than another. We observed that sessions with differing predominant foci had different moods. Therefore, we decided to subject the focusing issue to some experimental scrutiny. Finding nothing about the levels of intervention in the research on group psychotherapy, we decided to do some experimenting of our own.

Specifically, we wanted to know how the group responded to sessions which were predominantly focused on one level or another. What was the atmosphere in a person-centered (versus that in a couple, interpersonal, or group-as-a-whole) session? How did participants like the session? In which type of session was there more resistance? And in which type of session did the participants feel that they learned the most?

Procedures

For the purposes of this study, we wanted to assess the groups in the second working phase only. Thus, we made our assessments during a time at which the usual stage-determined crisis had been overcome but before termination issues had been raised.

The second part of the session is very highly influenced by the structured activity and is, therefore, subject to leader manipulation. Therefore, we decided to research only the first part of the session in which the influence of the leaders is less direct and the group as a whole exerts a strong influence on the focus of its work. For this reason, we gave the assessment instrument after the first half of each session for several weeks during the spring of 1989. Three different groups participated; a total of 14 sessions was evaluated.

Instrument

The tool we used to investigate the group's atmosphere is a modification of the Group Climate Questionnaire, Short Form GCQ-S (MacKenzie, 1983). The upper section of the tool is an exact replication of the GCQ-S. At the bottom we added three questions dealing with the degree to which the participants enjoyed the session, the amount of learning they believed they obtained in it, and the type of session it was in their opinion—person-centered (a), couple-centered (b), interpersonal (c), or group-as-a-whole (d). The form is reprinted in Appendix A-3.

Data were analyzed by averaging the scores for the 14 sessions into the Grand Mean (see Table 1). They were also analyzed separately for the three

TABLE 1
Couples Group Process Research

		Loading	All 4 A-type Sessions	All 5 B-type Sessions	All Others	Grand Mean
Q1	liking/caring	I	4.4	4.6	4.3	4.4
Q2	understanding	I	3.1	4.6	4.5	4.1
Q3	avoidance	II	2.2	0.8	1.1	1.3
Q4	participation	I	3.8	4.6	4.0	4.2
Q5	dependence	II	2.3	3.4	2.8	2.8
Q6	anger	III	0.4	1.2	0.8	0.9
Q7	withdrawal	II	1.9	0.8	1.0	1.1
Q8	confrontation	I	2.5	3.5	3.6	3.2
Q9	conformity	II	1.3	1.1	1.4	1.3
Q10	distrust	III	1.2	0.0	0.4	0.5
Q11	self-disclosure	I	3.0	4.3	4.4	3.9
Q12	tension		2.4	1.9	1.2	1.9
Q13	liked session		3.4	4.0	3.5	3.6
Q14	therap. gain		2.1	3.3	3.0	2.8
	Factors:					
I	Engaged		3.4	4.3	4.2	3.9
II	Avoidance		1.8	0.9	1.2	1.2
III	Conflict		0.8	0.6	0.6	0.7

groups under study, for those four sessions which were perceived as person-centered (a-type) and the five couple-centered (b-type) sessions. The averages are given for each item of the GCQ-S and for the three factors proposed by MacKenzie (1983). Table 1 indicates which item entered into which factor.

Findings

Of the three groups (CGA, CGB, and CGSH), one was assessed six times, one five times, and one only three times. Very few differences between the three groups emerged. No tests of significance were attempted because the research was too informal for such procedures. The data show that the predominant focus of a session had a much stronger influence on the group climate than the particular group of people present. Thus, while a group may have a generally slightly higher level of liking or avoidance than others, the impact of the subject matter in a given session was much more powerful.

As Table 1 shows, most of the sessions studied were perceived by the group members as predominantly person-focused (four sessions) or couple-focused (five sessions). The number of interpersonal (one session) and group-as-a-whole (one session) focused groups were too small to figure into the analysis.

It is also worth noting that there usually was a very high degree of agreement on the perception of focus between the members and between members and leaders. However, there were some interesting exceptions: On two occasions members and leaders were divided (a-type and b-type mix); on one there was a mix of opinions running the gamut.

Conclusions

Overall, group members in this study are expressing a very positive attitude towards their group at this developmental stage. They are engaged in their work, express liking for each other, and see anger and distrust as minimal. This good feeling arises partly from the character and spirit of these groups and partly from their being studied in their "best" developmental phase.

In the choice between person focus and couple focus, the data show a clear preference of the groups for couples work. In the couple-focused sessions — as opposed to person-centered ones—members felt more engaged and less avoidant. They liked the sessions better and felt that they gained more from them. A closer analysis of the raw data shows, not surprisingly, that those couples who were the focus of attention saw themselves as gaining more than the others. This explains why in these sessions there was a generally high degree of understanding (4.6 on a five-point scale) and engagement (4.3), yet only a moderate perception of therapeutic gain (3.3), indicating that nearly all couples felt active and energized in these sessions but only the ones who were the center of attention felt that they gained a great deal therapeutically.

It is, therefore, reasonable to conclude that of the two focal variations studied here the couples focus is more successful in creating a therapeutic group climate. Unfortunately, the data were insufficient to study the effects of interpersonally oriented and group-as-a-whole level sessions. These are fertile areas for further research. Moreover, it appears worthwhile to examine the group climate in different developmental phases as they become modified by the different levels of intervention.

9.
Handling Predictable Problems in Ongoing Groups

I have to be really married before I can leave the marriage, because how can you leave if you aren't really married? So, I'm going to learn what it means to be married and then, I may leave. Or perhaps I'll get really married.

—Nell

In order to keep a therapy group vibrant and effective the therapists must be prepared to handle a variety of problems which arise during the group's development. Many of these are familiar to every group therapist and seem to "come with the territory" of group therapy. Other types of problems, however, are indigenous to *couples* groups. In this chapter we discuss problems of both kinds and possible solutions.

HANDLING ROUTINE ISSUES AND MINOR MISHAPS

Many emergencies and serious group problems happen because minor difficulties and annoyances are not handled well. Therefore, dealing with the early warnings of impending trouble keeps a group functioning and fluid. The kinds of leadership decisions which later have a profound impact often seem less than grand strategic interventions. More often, they are comprised of many small decisions in a group's life. Catching a mistake before it gets big can prevent later trouble.

In Chapter 6, we mentioned Skip, who skipped out to a baseball game in May, forcing the group to deal with his absence in both his marriage and the group rather than face issues of recontracting and termination. We noted that this kind of regression occurs repeatedly at this phase of development and the astute reader may be wondering why we didn't prevent the problem from occurring. We overlooked it. The warning signs were there: Skip had begun to brag about his terrific attendance record, he was resisting discussing termination, he was resisting discussing any problems at all. But we overlooked it, and the group paid the price. Had we caught the problem, we could have worked with the group as a whole to educate them about Skip being in danger of acting out the group's resistance to facing the ending of the group. Had the group dealt with the issue as a unit, Skip would not have needed to leave as he did.

Routine issues and minor mishaps fall naturally into a number of categories:

1. Physical setting.
2. Absences.
3. Lateness.
4. Finances.

1. Physical Setting

Group members deserve a setting which is visually attractive and physically comfortable. Excessive heat or cold, intrusive noise, or uncomfortable seats create distractions which keep a group from maximal functioning and ultimately detract from group cohesiveness. It is helpful to have nearby bathroom facilities and a small kitchen for coffee or water. Some group therapists might disagree with the idea of providing amenities like coffee or tea; our experience has shown us that it serves to create an aura of safety and thus enhances cohesiveness.

Our group rooms were designed to have the atmosphere of a living room. We believe that this ambience helps to get the group going because it gives a message that the group room is a place in which people can safely make disclosures about themselves. It is a kind of "snug harbor" which is part of the larger world, yet psychologically removed from it. It is a room in which people are expected to know themselves and each other very, very well.

2. Absences

There are two kinds of absences: necessary absences and unnecessary absences. There will necessarily be absences since they are to be expected in a group of high-functioning individuals over an 11-month span of time. Most people are actually absent very little, but many adults must be out of town on occasion. We expect about two such absences per year for each couple and tell the couples so beforehand. A necessary absence is therefore dealt with as a routine matter. We request that people tell the group if they know in advance they will be out of town for an upcoming session.

When a member is ill, group members often write a get well card during the session, using the paper, crayons, and stickers we have on hand for such purposes. The attending spouse transmits the card and well-wishes. This adds to the cohesiveness of the group and to the missing member's feeling of belonging. Members tell us that this kind of thoughtfulness means a lot to them.

An unnecessary absence is of more clinical concern and will be discussed later in this chapter under "emergencies." When a member is absent with a superficial excuse — for example, that a Monday Night Football game is more important than the group — we consider this a group emergency and deal with it accordingly.

3. Lateness

Lateness in a couples group usually involves a couple, since most couples travel to the session together. We also find, paradoxically, that people with a tendency to be late marry people who insist on being on time or even early. Because of this dynamic, the couple which comes late more than once usually raises it as a problem. It is usually the time-conscious partner who is troubled by it and is likely to have the group's sympathy, since punctuality is desired group behavior. Lateness becomes a topic of discussion, sometimes accompanied by the laughter of recognition by other couples who gain an understanding of their own partner's behavior from other group members who identify with the partner. People who come late may hate to sit around and wait for things to start, while those who need to be on time may have been raised in an environment (family or school) in which lateness was severely punished. The discovery of these causes and the discussion of responsibility and time management in earlier family times often lead to greater appreciation of the partner's discomfort and frequently eases the lateness problem.

Latecomers gain a better understanding of their spouses' anxiety and feeling. It also helps the latecomers to hear from the group what went on while the group was waiting: Often, the couple in question have no idea that sitting in the waiting room before the meeting and engaging in pre-group socializing is fun and that, in fact, they are missing something by being late.

More important, group members let the late couple know — perhaps even with anger — that their lateness has kept the group from getting started and that it creates a waste of time and money for the people who are present. The leader will utter a totally confusing phrase, "The group starts when the last member is accounted for." Most of the time, the late couple had not considered the importance of time management in building an intimate relationship.

Thus, the group issue acts as a microcosm of relationship issues both between the partners and between the member and the world at large.

4. Finances

The full monthly fee is due on the first day of that month. If a couple have not paid by the second session of the month, the leader who is the "keeper of the structure" mentions this at the beginning of the second session. Couples know ahead about this procedure and instances of late payment are rare. When it is necessary to make late payment a group issue, the discussion is not set up as a public flogging, but as a therapeutic issue which increases understanding of the motivation for the nonpayment. Since a couple can simply request an extension of payment when needed by discussing the reason with the leader, we are able to distinguish between carelessness, actual financial hardship, and a couples or group issue.

A couple who falls behind in payment repeatedly probably does so because the handling of money is a clinical issue with that couple. A discussion which gets started due to unpaid fees can often help this couple and others in the group deal with the complexities of couples' financial management in a clinically valuable manner. Once again, the resentment of group members about "wasting time" when discussing carelessness in finances is quickly interpreted as a way in which carelessness engenders hostility in a relationship.

If a couple is unable to pay because of some unforeseen financial disaster, we do make arrangements for extending credit or for a reduction in the fee. However, in keeping with the trust in a good working relationship, these arrangements need to be made when the difficulty occurs, not when the couple is already in arrears and a group is annoyed at their nonpayment.

DEALING WITH NATURALLY EMERGING MEMBER ROLES IN THE GROUP

Member roles are naturally emerging group phenomena. In the course of interactions in the group, each member behaves in such ways that the group begins to expect this behavior from the member. The behavior always satisfies certain group needs, such as avoidance of a tough issue or comic relief, so that the member's behavior is rewarded by the whole group or by some segment in it. Group roles emerge from the systemic interaction between member and group. In a group, it is likely that if a particular member did not take a role, someone would be "elected" by the group to fulfill a given function.

A group role is the set of behavioral expectations placed upon an individual member to behave in certain predictable ways, which in turn allow the group to deal with this member in accordance with the expectation.

A number of excellent descriptions of typical group roles have been presented in the literature (Bogdanoff & Elbaum, 1978). The following discussion focuses on those naturally emerging member roles which we have encountered most frequently as they unfold in couples groups:

1. The Scapegoat.
2. The Joker.
3. The Polite Socializer.
4. The Monopolizer.
5. The Competitor.
6. The Would-be Co-leader.
7. "I'm just here for my spouse."

1. The Scapegoat

The scapegoat is usually the recipient of the group's anger at any time in its development. He/she has some kind of abrasive behavior which irritates other members, who either become angry in the group or smolder. The scapegoat provides a convenient target onto which to unload anger which might be more properly directed elsewhere, like at the leader, the partner, or the whole group. Most of the time, the behavior stops or the group learns to deal with it and goes on to the next developmental stage. Sometimes, however, the scapegoat is in danger of getting stuck in the role and the leader needs to intervene. This can be done either by making the process conscious and pointing out what is going on or by "reframing" — providing the group with a new way of looking at the scapegoating phenomenon. Although the scapegoat can be a member or a couple, it is most frequently one member of a couple.

Ted had been annoying a number of group members with his witty comments which were often unrelated to the matter at hand. For example, Ted liked movies. When someone in the course of making a point about his marriage would mention a certain movie, Ted would interrupt with comments about the movie. Instead of allowing the group to pounce on Ted and distance him further from the group, since he was shaky both in his self-esteem and in his commitment to the group, the leaders provided a reframing by pointing out some of the group issues. We pointed out that Ted, the scapegoat, was performing an important group function. He was keeping the group from moving too fast into uncharted waters, a concern which some other members shared. Thus, his shenanigans served to divert the group's attention from the unsettling issues it needed to address.

2. The Joker

The joker protects the group from anxiety by deflecting it through humor. While the group needs some comic relief, at times, in order not to be paralyzed by the anxiety in the room, it is the role of effective leaders, to supply this relief, which is very different from the part played by a joker.

The joker's "funny" remarks are not usually well-timed. They are often interruptive and not warmly received by the group. They seem out of place or too frequent. Yet much of the time the group rewards the joker's behavior with laughter. It is only when someone in the group has the courage to intervene and to ask the joker to tone things down that the joking diminishes and the group can return to serious work. At times, an intervention from the leaders is needed; when that is the case, it signifies that the joker has too much latent support in the group because the group as a whole is resisting work. At times, a request from the group for the joker to settle down does not suffice and stronger confrontation of the joker is needed. In this case the joker's behavior is more clearly characterologically determined and less of a temporary group phenomenon. Some therapeutic work on the origins of the behavior is necessary for things to settle down.

3. The Polite Socializer

This role is more frequently seen in a couples group than in other adult psychotherapy groups. Socializing and making polite conversation with other couples is, after all, part of a couple's social identity. Thus, the polite socializer is usually a well-meaning person who does not yet understand or is afraid to understand that a different type of behavior is expected in group psychotherapy. This person was often raised in a home in which one lived by the motto: "If you don't have anything nice to say in social circles don't say anything."

We head trouble off by educating prospective members about the difference between group psychotherapy and social conversation. We also teach the group to make a clear distinction between the conversation which goes on in the waiting room before the session and the ongoing group work in the session. We sometimes liken the hall to a kind of tunnel through which a person passes and becomes transformed into a working group member until passage back to the waiting area. Often, a group still opens a session with a few minutes of social banter. We do not participate in this banter because we do not want to send confusing messages to the members about desirable within-group behavior. After a few minutes of social conversation, one couple usually gets things going with a real issue. If the banter goes on too long, we provide an interpretation of its content or comment that the group is avoiding its task.

The polite socializer is someone who, despite the leaders' educational efforts, still does not understand the difference between group work and chatter. If the group is in a state of anxiety and avoidance, it may well support the socializing. More often, however, group members will become impatient and push the group back to its task, disregarding the polite socializer's chitchat in a more or less polite manner.

4. The Monopolizer

This is usually an anxious and needy member, who takes a large portion of the group's "air time" in a whining but authoritarian manner. Content varies from engaging the therapists in frequent lengthy debates to presenting a stream of narratives which are meant to illustrate a point but keep the attention focused on that member. Psychologically, the monopolizer is a needy child who is unable to share parental attention with other siblings, who needs to dominate the group and is resistant to the leaders' efforts. The monopolizer attracts the group's attention in an abrasive and nonconstructive manner and is in danger of becoming a scapegoat if the behavior continues unchecked.

In order to handle the monopolizer, we suggest involving the group in a planned intervention based on the leaders' assessment of the underlying interpersonal dynamic. One needs to be careful, however, that involving the group does not push the monopolizer into a scapegoat role.

> Jack had preoccupied his group for several sessions through complicated debates with other members and the leaders. Frequently, he would "hold forth" about his moral convictions and would expound tenaciously that the group had no right to try to get him to change them. Group members became exasperated with his lectures, but were actually steamrollered in their attempts to stop them.
>
> Just when this behavior had reached crisis proportions and Jack was in danger of becoming the group's scapegoat, the time for the annual workshop arrived. With an eye on the problem of Jack and on other couples' struggle with change, the group—encouraged by the leaders—choose "Changing and the Fear of Change" as the workshop theme. By participating in several exercises which dealt with his simultaneous desire to change the dynamic of his marriage and his resistance to the change, Jack became readier to accept the forward movement of the group and of his marriage. His monopolizing behavior lessened noticeably, which we considered progress. After all, a character trait as central as this one is not easily extinguished.

5. The Competitive Member

Competitive behavior can be expressed by interruptions like "Oh, that happened to me, too," a remark which upstages others rather than expressing empathy. Competitiveness can be seen in giving feedback which criticizes another member instead of expressing a feeling. At times, competitiveness arises between the partners in a couple, at other times between group members, and at times it goes from member to leader. Appropriate interventions include labeling the behavior for the group ("John, you sound like you are in competition with Jim") and relating it to family of origin issues.

If competitive behavior in the group is frequent, especially between the same two people, it is advisable for the leaders to look at their own dynamics and assess whether they are competing with each other and whether their competitiveness is repeating itself isomorphically in the group.

6. The Would-Be Co-Leader

This member, frequently a mental health professional needing couples therapy, is able to offer incisive observations and helpful comments to other members. But, as we know, it is hard for therapists to become patients. Other group members usually respond positively at first and express gratitude and admiration for all the expertise and help. After a while, however, it becomes clear that the helpfulness and profound insights act as a shield behind which the member hides, thereby being protected from self-disclosure and the need to work on one's own marital issues. The leader can intervene by making the process conscious to the person in question. Just as frequently, however, another group member will express dissatisfaction at the lack of personal openness of the would-be co-leader and the group begins to apply pressure on the pseudo-therapist to be a full group member.

> Dr. William George teaches psychology, but needed help in his marriage. He pontificated to his wife Bea. When he joined the group, members were at first dazzled with his insights. He said, "Couples often run into difficulty in the seventh year of marriage." The leaders were not making these grand statements, so the group assumed Dr. George was a leader, perhaps even more knowledgeable than the actual leaders. Dr. George secretly agreed. For the first two sessions, the group gloried in the education it was receiving about couples. Then they realized that they knew precious little about the William George behind the Dr., and began to feel like Bea in the marriage — lectured and condescended to, but not loved or respected. That was the beginning of William George's struggle to reveal the person inside, shy, insecure, and afraid that he was unlovable.

There are various styles of pseudo-leadership: effective and ineffective. Effective pseudo-leadership goes undetected longer since the member is able to integrate helpful comments and insights into the member role, seems modest, and phrases comments well. In contrast, the ineffective would-be co-leader makes observations which are ill-phrased, ill-timed, and presented in a showy or pompous manner. After some initial gratitude, the group usually resents and rejects these "interventions" and the member is in danger of losing the respect of the group unless the behavior is modified.

7. "I'm Just Here For My Spouse"

This occurs in a couple in which one spouse has carried the symptom for the marital unit. At first, there is collusive denial as both members agree that one of them is "sick" and in need of help while the other is mentally healthy. They also collude in denying the existence of a marital problem. Although the denial is not pervasive enough to prevent them from signing up for the group, it still impels the spouse to come into the first group session and proclaim to the group: "I'm just here for my spouse. The marriage is fine and so am I." The group is rarely fooled and sees its work cut out for it.

A group will not put up with this for long. After a few sessions, the supposedly "healthy" spouse is likely to be confronted on a behavior which exacerbates the other spouse's symptoms. If done with sufficient firmness, tact, and concurrent support for the member in question, the confrontation can turn the reluctant fence-sitter into a full-fledged member little by little over the ensuing months, as described earlier (Chapter 3) for Catherine and Todd.

HANDLING OF CLINICAL EMERGENCIES

Unlike the minor mishaps described above which happen in most couples groups and can be handled by straightforward interventions, emergencies require concentrated effort by and cooperation between the leaders, their staff, and the group. In the following section, we will describe some common clinical emergencies and possible responses to them.

Resistance By No-Show

Why do members fail to appear for a session? Although rare, this behavior usually occurs because a spouse is so angry at the partner and so disgusted with the marriage that he/she believes that the group is worthless since it is not helping the spouse to "shape up." Alternatively, the member may be suspicious that the group is siding with the spouse in the recurrent marital disputes. When this happens, the member may not show for the group session or be absent with a very lame "excuse." The spouse is likely to come in and tell the group of the events leading up to this nonappearance.

A situation like this calls for a very definitive and active intervention from the leaders and from the individual couples therapist. The couple clearly is in a crisis. If no help is given at this point, the couple might be lost to the group, much to the detriment of everyone involved. We suggest that the keeper of the structure place a call to the absent member while the group is meeting and discuss the situation immediately. This has happened only once in our five years, and was described in Skip's skipping out to a baseball game.

A more serious no-show situation would be one in which both partners refuse to come to a session. This has not happened in our own experience. We would schedule an emergency therapy session with the missing couple before the next group session and discuss the whole matter. We can imagine two kinds of situations which might lead to a rebellious no-show of a couple:

First, when it is still early in the group's development the non-appearance could be due to a couple's anxiety over being in the group. Careful preparation of the couples usually prevents this problem. If it happens, the couple's concerns need to be addressed. Perhaps they need more reassurance before they feel comfortable with being in a group. We suggest individual couples work to stem the crisis.

Second, it has occurred that near the middle stage of the group a couple was very dissatisfied with the group's progress. We strongly encouraged the couple to come into the group and raise their feelings of discomfort and dissatisfaction as a problem. This couple came close to leaving the group, and would have had the issue been handled defensively by the group and the leaders.

> One day during the fourth month of a group year Ben came to his auxiliary therapy session and complained bitterly about the group. He thought that the group was being too chatty and superficial and therefore progressing too slowly. He believed that he was wasting his money and mentioned that he and his wife were considering dropping out. The therapist, who also was one of the leaders, conveyed to Ben that she was taking his concerns seriously, that she was, in fact, in agreement with him, and that she wanted him to bring it up in group.
>
> Ben, who was in therapy because of his passivity, elected himself to be the spokesperson for the couple. Because he saw himself as a shy person and found it difficult to assert himself, this was therapeutically on target. Much to his surprise and delight, several members of the group agreed with his concern when he raised it. Not only did this move the group forward, but it also became a pivotal event for Ben, who continued to make progress in his quest for greater assertiveness. He understood the value of the task and could think in a multilevel way about its significance for himself, his marriage, and the group.

Breaking of Rules

Breaking of rules can occur at any time in the life of a group and has to be handled immediately. Letting things slide undermines the viability of the group and can lead to irreversible damage. Naturally, there are differences in the types of rules which are being broken; some are more serious than others. Breaking of a serious rule, such as breach of confidentiality, is a rare occurrence. Minor infractions, such as lateness, are more common and therapists are well served to have mechanisms in place to deal with these. More important incidents, like blatant socializing outside of the group or refusal to finish out the group year, require more than just mechanisms.

The therapist must use all the therapeutic skill and the power of the group itself to deal with the problem. Occasionally, it is advisable to call in a consultant. In other instances—for example, if confidence has been betrayed—it may be necessary to discharge a couple from the group and from the services of that therapist. If members can apologize to the group, the relationship may be reparable, and the group would be handled like a group in a crisis. Leaders must remain aware that such crises have long-range impact on the group and are better prevented than dealt with after the fact.

Divorce Threats and Impending Divorce

Occasionally a group contains a couple in which one or both partners verbalize thoughts or plans of divorce. What makes this an emergency is that the couple which repeatedly threatens divorce seriously undermines the morale of the group.

In many ways a divorce in a couples group is analogous (albeit not quite as disturbing) to a suicide in a non-couple therapy group. The marriage—which is, after all, the "primary patient" in the couples group—ceases to exist. If a couple were to go through with a divorce during the group year, they would have to leave the group.

Similar to suicide threats, divorce threats come in two varieties: acute and chronic. The acute threat occurs at the height of a crisis, with one or both partners extremely upset and despondent. The therapist needs to verbalize that—as long as they *want* to—the partners can resolve this crisis. The full support from the group can often turn the crisis around and restore a couple's sense of competence in overcoming trouble spots. It is extremely important that the group not take sides. It is very tempting for a group to see the villain and the victim in a divorcing couple. Getting hooked into such a pattern is likely to antagonize one partner—or even both—and worsen the divorce threat rather than lessen it.

The chronic divorce threat is a different matter. We all know couples who utter such threats repeatedly, but somehow no one takes it quite seriously. The group knows that these threats are a common occurrence and that neither partner is really willing or able to live without the other. In some couples, the divorce-threatening partner is always the same one and in all likelihood is using the threats as a tool of power against the other. In other couples, the partners actually take turns making the divorce threats, which are then part of a continuing dance of avoiding intimacy.

> Morris and Leslie had been coming to the group for some time and reported in each session some fight which ended in one of them threatening divorce. While this was quite unsettling to the group, which therefore spent a lot of time working with this couple, it did not sound like a threat which would come true soon. There were too many positive aspects to the marriage and too many fears of divorce on both sides. What was clear was that neither had good marital problem-solving skills and that both—like their parents before them—were using divorce threats to gain the upper hand in a fight. It further became clear that both partners—due to harrowing earlier life experiences—were afraid of true intimacy and avoided it by creating distance through the divorce threats.
>
> The group helped them to become less afraid of intimacy by working through some of their past history and it helped them to solve marital problems in a more constructive fashion. At one point, one of us elected to use a strategic maneuver by having both partners sign a contract not to use divorce threats for a whole month. This move was only partially successful. Both partners broke the agreement at least once, but it helped them to better understand the underlying dynamics and work on them instead of on the surface issues.

Handling the ongoing group is quite analogous to handling the routines of daily living in one's marriage, one's parenting experience, and one's career. Although the tried and true mechanisms for dealing with predictable trouble are reassuring and handy to have in place, one can never become too casual or comfortable in cavalierly handling group issues. As in life, people are sensitive to being "handled" and are likely to feel manipulated.

Skillful intervention is first and foremost done from the therapeutic stance of a genuine and caring human being. This stance, more than any of the techniques outlined above, enables a group to survive its developmental and daily bumps.

10.
Coordinating Clinical
Diagnosis with
Outcome Research

*We have learned to function better as individuals who are part
of a couple. We came to understand that being more comfortable as individuals reduced the pressure on the couple to provide individual identities.*

—*Dale*

Accountability for one's therapeutic work is an ethical obligation of our
profession (Salvendy, 1980). Therapists need to evaluate the work they do
and the procedures they employ in order to provide the best possible service,
to keep their skills honed, and to remain professionally viable. For this to
happen, there needs to be a careful assessment of the problem in the beginning,
intermittent checks on the progress, and a final evaluation of the treatment.

Since the assessments were already discussed in Chapter 1 and the intermittent checks on couples' progress were described in other chapters, this
present chapter will describe a small outcome study that we conducted with
clients who had participated in one or more years of couples groups.

OUTCOME RESEARCH ON PAST COUPLES GROUPS

Assessments made at the beginning of group participation form the basis
for later evaluations of a couple's progress and eventual success or failure in
therapy (Coché, 1983). Most of these evaluations are informal, though we do
not hesitate to bring a couple's initial Assessment Form into the last session of
a group and have the whole group evaluate how far a couple have come in
nearing the goals the partners had set.

In addition to these informal evaluations, we designed a small study,
described below, in which we sent questionnaires to couples who had com-

pleted couples groups in the past few years. As Marett (1988) points out, actual outcome research on couples groups is sparse and the few existing studies have serious methodological shortcomings. Still, we wanted answers to questions like: How effective are the groups? Assuming that they are effective, what are the particular areas of improvement as seen by the couples? Furthermore, in the eyes of the participants, what was it about the groups that made them effective for the couples? Following is a review of this study.

Goals and Objectives

The study was designed to offer a closer look at the outcome of the groups as perceived by former participants. Although we had received personal reports from the former members, we decided to take a look at the outcome question in a more systematic fashion.

Method

A brief questionnaire (see Appendix A-2) was sent to members who had participated in a couples group within the past three years. Of the 13 couples who received a questionnaire, nine returned it in time to be included in this analysis.

Instrument

We designed the questionnaire to approach the issue of therapeutic outcome from two angles: (1) What in the marriage is going better now and what is not? (2) What was there about the group that made it successful? We also added some questions regarding (1) the goal with which the couple entered the group and (2) ways to improve the couples group experience.

Results

The following table presents the average ratings of learning obtained in the group as received from the nine couples who responded (using a 3-point scale with 3 meaning most significant learning):

Communication	2.6
Fun	2.0
Knowing what it means to be a couple	2.4
Feeling closer to each other	2.2
More loving and intimate	2.7
Appreciate partner's individuality	2.7
Other	2.0

In the last category, one couple had learned as a result of observing the others in the group that its own problem was not so serious after all, but gave it a rating of 1, indicating that this bit of learning was insignificant. Another couple stated that they had learned a great deal about the other as an individual and rated it 3, or very meaningful.

The average rating of the next question about reaching one's personal goal was 4.0 on a 5-point scale with 5 as the highest, i.e. complete goal attainment. Goals included some typical couples issues like intimacy, sexual happiness, and communication. Other goals were more individual in nature, like an eating disorder, assertiveness, and wanting to be more organized. In fact, the large variety of goals was quite surprising.

Among the factors listed as most helpful about the group the following ratings were obtained on a 3-point scale (with 3 as the highest, or most helpful, rating):

Working in a group	2.7
Helping others	2.6
The therapists	2.7
Structured part of session	2.1
Unstructured part of session	2.6
Trust in people in group	2.6
Being honest	2.8
Knowing people cared	2.4
Concurrent nongroup therapy	2.6
Clear and written group policies	2.1
Other factors?	—

Other Learnings

We invited couples to tell us, in their own words, other learnings they had gained which they believe to be worthy of mention. Here are four couples' responses:

Paul and Amy: "We learned about each other as individuals and have appreciated each other more."

Jack and Deidre: "After we experienced honest and personalized contact with other couples the ratings of our problems diminished from 'this is a real big problem' to 'Aw, so what, no big deal.' "

Dale and Gerry: "We learned to accept our families of origin. Now, less energy is wasted on trying to 'fix' or change them, and more energy is left for us as a couple."

Will and Denise: "We do communicate more effectively and some of that
                    resulted from the group. . . . In some sense, we do know
                    more about being a couple. We both had definite individ-
                    ual issues which we tended not to look at. They were
                    clarified as part of the group."

The next question, regarding the type of couple who would benefit from
the group, was intended to approach the question of perceived benefits in an
indirect fashion. The general tenor of the responses indicates that in the view
of our respondents many couples could benefit from some work on their
communications, interpersonal skills, and/or intimacy issues. However, several couples mentioned that, in order to benefit from the group, couples need
to make a commitment to work on these issues.

The last question concerned ways to improve the group experience. It
generated a number of very thought-provoking write-in answers. Three couples suggested even greater therapist involvement, by which they meant
greater structuring of interventions by therapists at different points in the life
of the group. One couple wanted more answers from the therapists in general, one suggested more leader activity in the early phase of group development, one proposed more directiveness in the beginning phase of each
session. Two couples, who particularly liked the workshop formats, suggested
a workshop early on to build cohesiveness and suggested more structured
workshops in general.

Todd and Catherine represent the faction who resonate to structure and
guided learning: "We believe more therapist control earlier on in each session
would prevent a feeling of time restrictions at the end of each session. It's
great to let the group talk things through, but the therapists must control more
frequently and earlier for the optimal benefits for the couples."

Conclusions on Assessment and Evaluation

Couples told us that they received their greatest learning in the areas of
intimacy, communication, and the appreciation of one another's individuality.
Having more fun ranked surprisingly low. This could mean that having more
fun was not much of an issue before the couples joined, which is our observation,
or that we did not sufficiently attend to the issue in the groups. It certainly
deserves some thought.

Couples rated very high that they had achieved their initial goals and
later goals which they set during the course of the group. This is very
rewarding to the therapist. After all, the group is meant to help people make
changes in their desired direction. However, we also believe there is value in

looking at those couples who gave this a low rating and those who did not respond at all.*

Couples found the positive or cohesive tone of the group to be very helpful to them. Perceived as less helpful were structured exercises, despite the number of couples who requested more structured leader interventions. Here again, we need more data. We suspect that different individuals in the couples with different cognitive styles experience different kinds of leadership differently, and this seemingly contradictory set of data may, in fact, be due to different sub-groups responding consistently within their own experience. For example, couples like Catherine and Todd need and respond well to structure, while couples like Ben and Karen grow more quickly through the capacity to be involved in direct leadership behaviors in the group. Group policies were not viewed as helpful to the marriages of the members, nor would we expect them to be. In the eyes of the participants, the interpersonal aspects of the group were the most important: honesty, trust, helping and being in a group. The structure imposed by the therapists, important though it may be to the overall functioning of the group, is not paramount in the minds of the participants.

Asked how to improve the group, some couples, like Todd and Catherine, requested greater direction and leadership by the therapists. This presents an interesting therapeutic dilemma: Should we as leaders become more directive at the risk of making the group more dependent (Bion, 1960) or should we remain faithful to our theoretical concepts and let the group search for answers, believing, as we do, that people change when there is nothing left to do? If so, we will continue to invite the leadership behaviors to come from the group, even at the risk of being perceived as "wasting time" or "floundering" by members whose anxiety skyrockets at lack of evident structure. Although we believe that each therapy team has to find its own answers to this issue, any extreme in leadership style, either too laissez-faire or too autocratic, is likely to be detrimental to the group (Lewin, 1951).

Incorporating Research into Clinical Practice

As the studies in Chapters 8 and 10 show, research in the conduct of the groups does not have to be cumbersome, expensive, or esoteric. The studies reported here were accomplished with the help of a personal computer and a simple spreadsheet. Yet the results (though limited in their generalizability)

---

*We have had some contact with those who did not respond. One couple was disenchanted with us and with the group. Another couple separated but did not blame the group or the therapists. Two couples were satisfied and pleased with the group but "too busy" to fill out the questionnaire.

were extremely helpful to us in providing us with feedback on the work we are doing in the couples groups and in continuing to make adjustments in our treatment package. We encourage clinicians to build in similar modest but viable evaluations into their clinical service delivery. The feedback loop in letting consumers know that their psychotherapists are interested in their responses more than compensates for the inconveniences in collecting the data.

CONCLUDING THOUGHTS

We have taken the reader through the background, the inception, the literature, and the clinical practice of a unique model in couples group psychotherapy. The trip has been an adventuresome one for us as mental health professionals. It has enabled us to integrate theory, research, and practice from disciplines too often seen as unrelated and even, at times, in contradiction with one another. And yet, we believe that this marriage of ideas enriches the model in a manner which would be hard to replicate using one pathway alone. As marital partners, we found the experience of developing this model stimulating and creative, even when fraught with the inevitable differences of opinions which partnership brings. We are reminded of an inscription from a couple, both mental health professionals themselves, in a book which they gave us at our wedding: "We wish for you, in your marriage, many levels of creativity." In conclusion, we wish our colleagues many levels of their own creativity as they work with couples in groups.

Appendices

Appendix A: Assessment and Outcome Tools

APPENDIX A-1

Couples Assessment Inventory

Instructions: Each member of the couple is to take 45 minutes to respond to the questions below. Thereafter, take one hour to discuss the issues together.

1. Reflect on two qualities in your partner which motivated you to choose him/her.

    1a. How has each quality withstood the test of time?

1b.   How do you react to each quality?

2.   List two major problems in your relationship which cause you pain and unhappiness.

   2a.   How have you personally worked with your partner to "solve" the problems?

   2b.   What has been your partner's reaction to your attempts?

3.   Name two personal goals which you, as an individual, have for yourself in the near future.

3a.   How would achieving this goal impact on your relationship with your partner?

4.   Reflecting on your parent's marriage(s), comment on one major similarity between your style as a partner and that of your parent(s).

4a.   How does your partner's response (to that similar style) compare with that of your parents?

5.   Name one way in which you are determined to make your relationship different from your parents' marriage(s).

5a.   What strategies do you employ?

5b.   How does your partner react?

APPENDIX A-2

Couples Psychotherapy Group
Follow-up Questionnaire, Summer, 1989

Directions: Set aside 30 minutes with your partner. Read each question aloud. Discuss your answer and write answers which both of you agree on as a couple. Add comments or vignettes on separate sheet(s) of paper if you wish.

1. Below are learnings or gains which couples have told us they received from the couples group experience. Rate each item as it applies to you as a couple, using a 3-point scale:

> 1 = not so or not much
> 2 = somewhat more than before
> 3 = definitely better than before

[   ] We communicate more effectively in conflict areas
[   ] We have more fun together than when we joined
[   ] We know more about what it means to be a couple
[   ] We feel closer to each other as people, more real, more honest, more human
[   ] We feel more loving and intimate with one another more of the time
[   ] We appreciate each other's individuality more
[   ] Other learnings? Please use extra paper

2. Reflecting on the major goal(s) for your relationship which motivated you to join the couples group, to what extent have you approached these goals? Circle the number which best applies to you as a couple.

> 1. Not at all
> 2. A bit
> 3. Somewhat
> 4. A good deal
> 5. Nothing is perfect, but this is terrific

What were your goals, as you remember them?
MAJOR GOAL (man):

MAJOR GOAL (woman):

3. Below are a list of factors which people find helpful in psychotherapy. Rate each, to the degree it was helpful to you as a couple. Write in the number which best applies:

> 1 = not at all helpful
> 2 = somewhat helpful
> 3 = very helpful

[   ] Working with your partner in a group of couples
[   ] Working with, helping other couples in the group
[   ] The therapists in the group
[   ] The structured parts of the couples group
[   ] The unstructured part of the couples group
[   ] Being able to trust people in the group
[   ] Being honest about what was wrong
[   ] Knowing people cared about your welfare
[   ] Therapy concurrent with the group
[   ] Clear and written group policies
[   ] Other factors? Please use extra paper

4. To whom would you recommend the couples group? Why? What can a couple expect to get out of it?

5. Can you think of ways we can improve the experience? What would you suggest?

APPENDIX A-3

Group Climate Questionnaire (GCQ-S)*
(MacKenzie, 1983)

Name _____

Group _____

Date _____

Instructions: *Read each statement carefully and try to think of the group as a whole. Using the Rating Scale as a guide, circle the number of each statement which best describes the group during today's session.* **Please mark only ONE answer for each statement.**

RATING SCALE	
0	not at all
1	a little bit
2	somewhat
3	moderately
4	quite a bit
5	a great deal
6	extremely

1. The members liked and cared about each other.
0 1 2 3 4 5 6

2. The members tried to understand why they do the things they do, tried to reason it out.
0 1 2 3 4 5 6

3. The members avoided looking at important issues going on between themselves.
0 1 2 3 4 5 6

4. The members felt what was happening was important and there was a sense of participation.
0 1 2 3 4 5 6

5. The members depended upon the group leader(s) for direction.
0 1 2 3 4 5 6

6. There was friction and anger between the members.
0 1 2 3 4 5 6

7. The members were distant and withdrawn from each other.
0 1 2 3 4 5 6

8. The members challenged and confronted each other in their efforts to sort things out.
0 1 2 3 4 5 6

9. The members appeared to do things the way they thought would be acceptable to the group.
0 1 2 3 4 5 6

10. The members distrusted and rejected each other.
0 1 2 3 4 5 6

11. The members revealed sensitive personal information or feelings.
0 1 2 3 4 5 6

12. The members appeared tense and anxious.
0 1 2 3 4 5 6

(continued)

*The questionnaire as presented here has been modified by the authors with the addition of statements 13, 14, and 15. The GCQ-S, was reprinted with permission from MacKenzie (1983).

GCQ-S Modification by Coché and Coché

13. I liked today's session   0 1 2 3 4 5 6
14. I gained therapeutically from this session   0 1 2 3 4 5 6
15. Today's session was mostly focused on: (circle one letter)

    A.   an individual (or individuals)
    B.   a couple (or couples)
    C.   the relations (similarities, interactions) between members in the group
    D.   The whole group (e.g. group rules, decisions, leadership issues, termination . . .)

Appendix B:
Examples of Types
of Structured Exercises

Following are examples of various types of structured exercises, along with responses by actual group members to the exercises, where applicable.

GUIDED IMAGERY: THE FALSE ALARM

The following exercise was presented to the workshop participants at the American Association of Marriage and Family Therapy workshop in San Francisco, October, 1989. The workshop was held at the Annual Conference, which took place six days after a major earthquake hit the San Francisco Bay area. The exercise is exactly what we would have done in a couples group that week, had there been one in San Francisco. It represents a multilevel healing way to deal with the existential disaster which the earthquake presented.

Sit comfortably so that your feet are supported by the floor and your arms and hands are supported by your body. Rest your head on a back or head rest or on the muscles of your neck by letting it hang forward slightly. Breathe deeply, concentrating on the wonder of your breath as it enters and leaves your body. Close your eyes as I take you on a special journey . . . a journey to a place inside you where meaning occurs . . . where people are important . . . where what is most important becomes clear and graspable.

As you concentrate on the sound of my voice and on your breathing, you may drift in and out of a slightly different way of being in the world. Your fingers may tingle. You may seem to be dozing off. Allow yourself to know that you are safe with us here to explore yourself. You will remember everything that happens and it can guide you to being more in touch with what is so important to you and to those you love.

Imagine that you are sitting comfortably at the kitchen or dinner table with someone you love . . . your spouse, your children, your lover, your friend, your parents, your brother or sister. It is a typical family meal for you . . . you are sitting in the presence of those you love . . . If you live alone, imagine that you have invited someone to dine with you . . . someone you love and value. Take a moment to look at the faces of those at the table. How old are they? How are they dressed? What do their faces tell you of how they are feeling at this normal dinner-time conversation? What are they talking about? What is the mood at the table? Are people seriously involved with one another? Is all attention focused on one person? Take a moment to notice, to be aware of how you feel towards these people with whom you share your evening meal.

Suddenly all is not well. Imagine a threat to your well-being . . . a hurricane approaches suddenly, a fire breaks out in an electric wire, a refrigerator emits poisonous gas, an earthquake tremor is suspected, a burglar seem to appear from nowhere with a gun. Suddenly something occurs which grips you in terror and in shock. A sudden danger to the well-being of those you love, and to the well-being of yourself and your belongings. Look now at the faces at the table and let yourself seek the threat of disaster. As you look at those who are at the table with you, allow yourself to feel the threat of loss, of death, of destruction, of property . . . the threat of an unknown terror. Take a moment now to let yourself know how much it means to you to cherish the friendship, or the love, of those with you. Think of what you would miss the most if the disaster were to strike. And now, just as you are coming to know the threat of loss, imagine that this was, after all, a false alarm.

The false alarm becomes clear to you now as you sit with your loved ones. The burglar was just a neighbor, the fire gets doused, the tremor passes by, the hurricane misses your house, the fire department is called for the gas leak. All is safe . . . imagine the threat lifting as you imagine how your disaster turns into merely a false alarm.

And now, with new vision, look at the faces of those with you. Imagine that you can touch, embrace, hug those near you. Imagine that you can tell your friend, your lover, your family about the pain of the imagined loss and the relief of the false alarm. Imagine that you have become aware, through the threat of disaster, of the treasured relationships in your life.

And finally, before you come back to be with us in this big room, promise yourself, when you go home from this remarkable journey which you have had this day in San Francisco . . . promise yourself that you will take the time to let those whom you love know that you took the time to notice how much they meant to you. Promise yourself, that from this threat of loss, you can become more intensely aware, and more expressively appreciative, of what in your self, your home, your work, and your beloved friends and family . . . of how much this gives you every single day of your life.

As I count backwards, come back into the room slowly. 9-8-7-6-begin to attend to cues in the room-5-4-3-wiggle your toes and fingers-2-1-and slowly open your eyes. Hello, everyone.

Discussion: It is imperative to have a chance to "debrief" after an intense experience like this. People will feel energized by talking themselves or by listening to others talk if time does not permit participation by everyone. Enable participants to discuss whatever they choose about their experience in the fantasy.

DIRECTED VERBAL SHARING: CHANGING AN ARGUMENT

Instructions: Think for a moment about one very specific and focused change you would like to make within your intimate relationship in the way in which you argue with your partner. After thinking about this, we will discuss it individually, with each couple comparing the changes they would like to make.

What the couples said:

Lena and Jared

Lena: When there is a topic we are arguing about, I'd like to find a way to help Jared to access his feelings more.

Jared: I'd like to stop seeing anger as a disaster. I'd actually like to be able to see intense feelings as an opportunity, like we have discussed in the group. I'd like to be more aware of how I censor my feelings.

Randy and Karl

Randy: I wish we could raise issues before they fester. I mean, I wish we could discuss problems before we do. I'd like to become more aware earlier that something is bothering me.

Karl: I need to change my passivity, to change my reluctance to initiate an argument when it is indicated, to be more confident in initiating things with Randy.

Skip and Nell

Nell: I need to say what I feel hurt by. I need to tell Skip when the way he speaks to me hurts me.

Skip: I need to be more up front with a problem that's bothering me. I need to speak up sooner. Not withdraw. Worry less about Nell's reaction.

WRITING EXERCISES: THE MEANING OF MARRIAGE

Instructions: Take a pencil and paper and write your quick response to the following question. You have about five minutes to write, before we discuss this together. For you as an individual, what does it mean to be married? Or, what would you like it to mean to be married?

What the couples wrote:

Karl and Randy

Karl: To take the whole package . . . because of the other person's good points and even because of the bad. To take care of each other. To be ever entwined with the other.

Randy: I would like it to mean constancy, planning together. Knowing we were making plans with the ground point assumption of continuing being together.

Skip and Nell

Nell: To be accepted as you are and then to be able to flex, to bend and to change, to blend more harmoniously with your partner's personality. To be able to share joy, pain and sorrow, without worrying about how you sound. To build a life together that is interesting to both. To care for each other and meet each other's needs. To forgive each other for hurtful indiscretions. To express love physically. To give each other room to grow as individuals. This is what I'd like marriage to be.

Skip: (Wrote nothing.)

Jared and Lena

Lena: To agree to a lifelong adventure and conversation.

Jared: A vote of confidence that this person and I will struggle with maintaining ourselves.

SOCIOGRAM ACTIVITIES

See Chapter 7.

DRAMATIC ACTIVITIES

See Chapter 7.

Appendix C:
Group Psychotherapy Policies at Coché and Coché

Introduction. The following policies have been adopted from those suggested by the American Group Psychotherapy Association, and provide a foundation by which group psychotherapy at Coché and Coché can function with maximum power. All are accepted and effective methods in handling psychotherapy in groups. We thank you in advance for honoring and respecting the points discussed below.

Written confidentiality agreement within the group. All information discussed in group psychotherapy meetings is to remain in the room. Names of other group members are not to be brought home to family or friends, and issues involving the lives of other group members are to be held in strictest confidence. In order to discuss one's own psychotherapy work, the best method is to relate the situation germane to yourself, pulling in other members anonymously and only as auxiliaries.

Confidentiality between members of a family. Members of the same family who are concomitantly in group psychotherapy and other forms (couple or family therapy) are not to discuss the happenings of the group in the other form of psychotherapy. Confidentiality between family members is left to the discretion of the psychotherapist. Confidentiality about the families of the group members which is gained through prior or simultaneous psychotherapy will be handled on a case by case basis.

Teaching and training release. We ask that you give us written permission to tape some sessions. This will usually be known in advance, and is taped by a visiting experienced clinician. The tape functions in two capacities: (1) It greatly augments the psychotherapy experience for the members. It is possible for a group or individual to schedule a special session at no charge or to use the tape in the ongoing psychotherapy group. This gives people the opportunity to see their nonverbal interactive style; (2) We are often asked to do teaching, training, clinical supervision, and professional writing about group psychotherapy. This is limited to a professional audience and often takes place outside of the Delaware Valley. Should anyone in the professional audience be familiar with anyone on the tape, they are asked ahead of time to leave the room, in order to maintain the integrity of the outside relationship.

Pre- and post-goal and symptom assessments. 1) Symptom assessments are administered at no charge at the beginning of, and sometimes after, the psychotherapy group. These should be filled out spontaneously and will be analyzed by the cotherapists. Feedback is available at no charge upon request. 2) Each member is requested to write what her/his goals are during the course of the upcoming clinical year. Reports on the progress of the client become part of the group work, and are used in planning for the potential leave-taking or continuation of the member the following year.

Group absences. The group takes place unless there is a holiday or both psychotherapists are out of the city. An attempt to reschedule the group for that week will be made. We assume that members will be absent from the group between two to four times in an 11-month period due to illness, vacation, or business conflicts. Lateness and superficial absences are dealt with by the working group.

Socializing. We request that during membership in a group you limit your social contact with other members. Please do not invite others for coffee, social gatherings, or to celebratory events. The group can plan ways to celebrate the accomplishments of its members as part of the group experience. We expect that after group sessions members may engage in social conversation on their way out of the building. We ask that discussion remain on the level of social conversation. Thus group psychotherapy issues are restricted to the time and location of the group meeting.

Special workshop. A special workshop of two to three hours may be held in May or June in Stone Harbor, New Jersey as part of the ongoing group experience. The topic is chosen at the request of the group members, and is decided in the spring.

Adjunctive individual, couples and family therapy. Although there may be very infrequent meetings with the therapist outside of the group times, it is necessary to have another form of therapy (couple, family, individual) available as a foundation. Group psychotherapy is a very lively opportunity to raise a number of issues, but time limitations may prevent dealing with issues in depth. Individual sessions are scheduled as decided by the outside therapist and the group member.

Fees. The monthly charge is payable at the first of the month. Statements are sent to each member at the end of the month for insurance and tax purposes. Because financial mismanagement is important in psychotherapy, tardiness in payment will be discussed within the group as needed.

The group therapy contract. Group psychotherapy in a group in which members begin and end together is based on members' trust in one another, that each will honor the full time and financial commitment. A breach of this contract against professional advice releases Coché and Coché from further responsibility to the client.

How to work in a group. Because of the richness of the experience, members will benefit from the group whether they sit back and listen or actively pursue issues of importance. It is our experience that the greatest benefit can be obtained by being as honest as possible as quickly as possible, and by talking up. Group therapists assist in forming a cohesive and trusting atmosphere so that maximum benefit can be obtained.

Alumni contacts. A natural outgrowth of membership in a Coché and Coché group can be to develop an interest in outside friendships once previous members are no longer active group participants. We ask that confidentiality be maintained about current group members and that "alumni" activities be reported to the Group Psychotherapy director. Current group members must limit social activity to one alumnus at a time, in order to avoid problems for other group members who also want to participate in alumni group activities. If a member is "taking time off" and may choose to return to a group at a later time, minimal socializing with members ensures the likelihood of a successful reentry into a current psychotherapy group.

Training function. Cotherapy is provided by trained professionals at a post-graduate level. Cotherapists are either staff psychologists or postgraduate interns doing advanced training in group psychotherapy. Each group has a consistent team of the same two professionals for each clinical year.

We thank you for your cooperation with these policies, and encourage you to discuss any questions or disagreements with the psychotherapist who is heading your group.

JUDITH COCHÉ, Ph.D.
Diplomate (Clinical), A.B.P.P.
Summer 1989

BIBLIOGRAPHY

Agazarian, Y., & Peters, R. (1981). *The Visible and Invisible Group: Two Perspectives on Group Psychotherapy and Group Process.* London: Routledge & Kegan Paul.

Bader, E., & Pearson, P. T. (1988). *In Quest of the Mythical Mate: A Developmental Approach to Diagnosis and Treatment in Couples Therapy.* New York: Brunner/Mazel.

Beck, A. T. (1979). *Cognitive Therapy and Emotional Disorders.* New York: New American Library.

Bennis, W., & Shephard, H. (1956). A theory of group development. *Human Relations, 9,* 415-437.

Bion, W. R. (1960). *Experiences in Groups.* New York: Basic Books.

Bloch, S., Browning, S., & McGrath, G. (1983). Humour in group psychotherapy. *British Journal of Medical Psychology, 56,* 89-97.

Bogdanoff, M., & Elbaum, P. (1978). Role lock: Dealing with monopolizers, mistrusters, isolates, "helpful Hannahs," and other assorted characters of group psychotherapy. *International Journal of Group Psychotherapy, 28,* 247-262.

Borriello, J. F. (1979). Intervention foci in group psychotherapy. In L. R. Wolberg & M. L. Aronson (Eds.), *Group Psychotherapy, 1979.* New York: Stratton Intercontinental.

Buber, M. (1958). *I and Thou* (2nd ed., R. G. Smith, Trans.). New York: Charles Scribner's Sons.

Bugental, J. F. T. (1981). *The Search for Authenticity: An Existential-Analytic Approach to Psychotherapy.* New York: Irvington Publishers.

Bugental, J. F. T. (1984). *The Art of the Psychotherapist: Evoking the Healing/Growth Potential.* Santa Rosa, CA: Psychology Corporation.

Cividini, E., & Klain, E. (1973). Psychotherapy in the cotherapeutic group. *Socijalna-Psihijatrija, 1,* 65-74.

Coché, E. (1983). Change measures and clinical practice in group psychotherapy. In R. R. Dies & K. R. MacKenzie (Eds.), *Advances in Group Psychotherapy* (pp. 79-99). New York: International Universities Press.

Coché, E., & Dies, R. R. (1981). Integrating research findings into the practice of group psychotherapy. *Psychotherapy: Theory, Research and Practice, 18,* 410-416.

Coché, E., Polikoff, B., & Cooper, J. (1980). Participant self-disclosure in group therapy. *Group, 4,* 28-35.

Coché, J. M. (1980). Social roles and family interaction in collaborative work. In E. A. Pepitone (Ed.), *Children in Cooperation and Competition: Toward a Developmental Social Psychology* (pp. 389-411). Lexington, MA: Lexington Books.

Coché, J. M. (1984). Psychotherapy with women therapists. In F. W. Kaslow (Ed.), *Psychotherapy with Psychotherapists* (pp. 151-169). New York: The Haworth Press.

Coché, J. M. (1990). Resistance in existential-strategic marital therapy. *Journal of Family Psychology, 3,* 236-250.

Coché, J. M., & Coché, E. (1986). Group psychotherapy: The severely disturbed patient in hospital. *Carrier Foundation Newsletter, 113,* 1-7.

Cooper, L. (1976). Co-therapy relationships in groups. *Small Group Behavior, 7,* 473-498.

Davis, K. L., & Meara, N. M. (1982). So you think it is a secret. *Journal for Specialists in Group Work, 7,* 149-153.

Dicks, H. V. (1967). *Marital Tensions: Clinical Studies Towards a Psychological Theory of Interaction.* New York: Basic Books, Inc.

Erikson, E. H. (1968). *Identity: Youth and Crisis.* New York: W. W. Norton & Company.

Flapan, D. (1981). Interventions of the group therapist. *Issues in Ego Psychology, 4,* 19-31.

Flapan, D., & Fenchel, G. H. (1983). Group member contacts without the group therapist. *Group, 7(4),* 3-16.

France, D. G., & Dugo, J. M. (1985). Pretherapy orientation as preparation for open psychotherapy groups. *Psychotherapy, 22,* 256-261.

Frankl, V. E. (1963). *Man's Search for Meaning: An Introduction to Logotherapy.* New York: Washington Square Press.

Fromm, E. (1956). *The Art of Loving.* New York: Harper & Row.

Gilligan, Carol. (1982). *In a Different Voice: Psychological Theory and Women's Development.* Cambridge, MA: Harvard University Press.

Gurman, A. S. (Ed.). (1985). *Casebook of Marital Therapy.* New York: The Guilford Press.

Hellwig, K., & Memmott, R. J. (1974). Co-therapy: The balancing act. *Small Group Behavior, 5,* 175-181.

Jacobson, N. S., & Gurman, A. S. (Eds.). (1986). *Clinical Handbook of Marital Therapy.* New York: The Guilford Press.

Kaufmann, W. (1975). *Existentialism from Dostoevsky to Sartre.* New York: Meridian.

Keeney, B. P., & Ross, J. M. (1985). *Mind in Therapy: Constructing Systemic Family Therapies.* New York: Basic Books.

Keeney, B. P., & Silverstein, O. (1986). *The Therapeutic Voice of Olga Silverstein.* New York: The Guilford Press.

Kirschenbaum, M. J., & Glinder, M. G. (1972). Growth processes in married-couples group therapy. *Family Therapy, 1,* 85-104.

Kluge, P. (1974). Group psychotherapy for married couples. *Psychotherapie und medizinische Psychologie, 24,* 132-137.

Kutash, I. L., & Wolf, A. (1983). Recent advances in psychoanalysis in groups. In H. I. Kaplan & B. J. Sadock (Eds.), *Comprehensive Group Psychotherapy* (pp. 132-138). Baltimore: Williams & Wilkins.

Langley, D. M., & Langley, G. E. (1983). *Dramatherapy and Psychiatry.* London: Croom Helm.

Lazarus, A. A. (1971). *Behavior Therapy and Beyond.* New York: McGraw-Hill.

Lederer, W. J., & Jackson, D. D. (1968). *The Mirages of Marriage.* New York: W. W. Norton & Company.

Leuner, H. (1969). Guided affective imagery: A method of intensive psychotherapy. *American Journal of Psychotherapy, 23,* 4-22.

Levinson, D. J., Darrow, C. N., Klein, E. B., Levinson, M. H., & McKee, B. (1978). *The Seasons of a Man's Life.* New York: Alfred A. Knopf.

Lewin, K. (1951). *Field Theory in Social Science: Selected Theoretical Papers.* Chicago: The University of Chicago Press.

Livesley, W. J., & MacKenzie, K. R. (1983). Social roles in psychotherapy groups. In R. R. Dies & K. R. MacKenzie (Eds.), *Advances in Group Psychotherapy* (pp. 117-135). New York: International Universities Press.

Low, P., & Low, M. (1975). Treatment of married couples in a group run by a husband and wife. *International Journal of Group Psychotherapy, 25,* 54-66.

MacKenzie, K. R. (1983). The clinical application of a group climate measure. In R. R. Dies & K. R. MacKenzie (Eds.), *Advances in Group Psychotherapy* (pp. 159-170). New York: International Universities Press.

MacKenzie, K. R., & Livesley, W. J. (1983). A developmental model for brief group therapy. In R. R. Dies & K. R. MacKenzie (Eds.), *Advances in Group Psychotherapy* (pp. 101-116). New York: International Universities Press.

Marett, K. M. (1988). A substantive and methodological review of couples group therapy outcome research. *Group, 12,* 241-246.

Mayerson, N. H. (1984). Preparing clients for group therapy: A critical review and theoretical formulation. *Clinical Psychology Review, 4,* 191-213.

McGoldrick, M., Anderson, C. M., & Walsh, F. (Eds.). (1989). *Women in Families: A Framework for Family Therapy.* New York: W. W. Norton & Company.

McGoldrick, M., & Gerson, R. (1985). *Genograms in Family Assessment.* New York: W. W. Norton & Company.

Meadow, D. (1988). Preparation of individuals for participation in a treatment group: Development and empirical testing of a model. *International Journal of Group Psychotherapy, 38,* 367-385.

Miller, J. B. (1976). *Toward a New Psychology of Women.* Boston: Beacon Press.

Moreno, J. L. (1951). *Sociometry, Experimental Method, and the Science of Society.* Beacon, NY: Beacon House.

Moreno, J. L., & Moreno, Z. T. (1959). *Psychodrama.* Beacon, NY: Beacon House.

Napier, A. Y., & Whitaker, C. A. (1978). *The Family Crucible: One Family's Therapy —An Experience that Illuminates All Our Lives.* New York: Bantam Books.

Neill, J. R., & Kniskern, D. P. (Eds.). (1982). *From Psyche to System: The Evolving Therapy of Carl Whitaker.* New York: The Guilford Press.

Nichols, K. A. (1976). Preparation for membership in a group. *Bulletin of the British Psychological Society, 29,* 353-359.

Nietzsche, F. (1960). *Also Sprach Zarathustra: Ein Buch fur Alle und Keinen.* München: Goldmann.

Nobler, H. (1986). When group doesn't work: An examination of the types and causes of individual, group, and leader failures. *Group, 10,* 103-110.

Ormont, L. R. (1981). Principles and practice of conjoint psychoanalytic treatment. *American Journal of Psychiatry, 138,* 69-73.

Papp, P. (1976). Family choreography. In P. J. Guerin (Ed.), *Family Therapy: Theory and Practice*. New York: Gardner Press.

Papp, P. (1982). Staging reciprocal metaphors in a couples group. *Family Process, 21,* 453-467.

Pfeiffer, J. W., & Jones, J. E. (1974). *A Handbook of Structured Experiences for Human Relations Training*. LaJolla: University Associates.

Pittman, F. (1989). *Private Lies: Infidelity and the Betrayal of Intimacy*. New York: W. W. Norton & Company.

Richman, J. (1979). A couples therapy group on a geriatric service. *Journal of Geriatric Psychiatry, 12,* 203-213.

Roback, H. B., & Smith, M. (1987). Patient attrition in dynamically oriented treatment groups. *American Journal of Psychiatry, 144,* 426-431.

Rogers, C. R. (1951). *Client-Centered Therapy: Its Current Practice, Implications, and Theory*. Boston: Houghton Mifflin Company.

Rogers, C. R. (1957). The necessary and sufficient conditions of therapeutic personality change. *Journal of Consulting Psychology, 21,* 95-103.

Rutan, J. S., Alonso, A., & Molin, R. (1984). Handling the absence of group leaders: To meet or not to meet. *International Journal of Group Psychotherapy, 34,* 273-287.

Rutan, J. S., & Stone, W. N. (1984). *Psychodynamic Group Psychotherapy*. New York: Macmillan Publishing Company.

Sager, C. J. (1976). *Marriage Contracts and Couple Therapy: Hidden Forces in Intimate Relationships*. New York: Brunner/Mazel.

Salvendy, J. T. (1980). Group psychotherapy training: A quest for standards. *Canadian Journal of Psychiatry, 25,* 394-402.

Sartre, J. P. (1948). *Intimacy* (L. Alexander, Trans.). New York: Avon Publications, Inc.

Sartre, J. P. (1948). *Existentialism and Humanism*. London: Methuen & Co., Ltd.

Satir, V. (1967). *Conjoint Family Therapy* (rev. ed.). Palo Alto: Science and Behavior Books, Inc.

Satir, V. (1988). *The New Peoplemaking*. Mountain View, CA: Science and Behavior Books.

Schein, E. H., & Bennis, W. G. (1965). *Personal and Organizational Change Through Group Methods*. New York: John Wiley & Sons.

Schwab, J., Baldwin, M., Gerber, J., Gomori, M., & Satir, V. (1989). *The Satir Approach to Communication: A Workshop Manual*. Palo Alto: Science and Behavior Books.

Selvini-Palazzoli, M., Boscolo, L., Cecchin, G. F., & Prata, G. (1980). Hypothesizing-circularity-neutrality: Three guidelines for the conductor of the session. *Family Process, 19,* 3-12.

Sherif, M., & Sherif, C. W. (1953). *Groups in Harmony and Tension*. New York: Harper & Row.

Sherif, M., & Sherif, C. W. (1969). *Social Psychology*. New York: Harper & Row.

Singer, J. L., & Pope, K. S. (1978). *The Power of Human Imagination*. New York: Plenum Press.

Spitz, H. I. (1979). Group approaches in treating marital problems. *Psychiatric Annals, 9,* 318-330.

Stone, E. (1988). *Black Sheep and Kissing Cousins: How Our Family Stories Shape Us.* New York: Times Books.

Thelen, H. (1954). *Dynamics of Groups at Work.* Chicago: University of Chicago Press.

Tillich, P. (1952). *The Courage to Be.* New Haven: Yale University Press.

Truax, C. B., & Carkhuff, R. R. (1967). *Towards Effective Counseling and Psychotherapy: Training and Practice.* Chicago: Aldine.

Vaillant, G. E. (1977). *Adaptation to Life: How the Best and the Brightest Came of Age.* Boston: Little, Brown and Company.

Vannicelli, M., Canning, D., & Griefen, M. (1984). Group therapy with alcoholics: A group case study. *International Journal of Group Psychotherapy, 34,* 127-147.

von Bertalanffy, L. (1968). *General System Theory: Foundations, Development, Applications.* New York: Braziller.

Walters, M., Carter, B., Papp, P. & Silverstein, O. (1988). *The Invisible Web: Gender Patterns in Family Relationships.* New York: The Guilford Press.

Watzlawick, P. (1978). *The Language of Change: Elements of Therapeutic Communication.* New York: Basic Books.

Watzlawick, P. (1983). *The Situation is Hopeless, But Not Serious: The Pursuit of Unhappiness.* New York: W. W. Norton & Company.

Watzlawick, P. (Ed.). (1984). *The Invented Reality: How Do We Know What We Believe We Know?* New York: W. W. Norton & Company.

Watzlawick, P., Weakland, J. H., & Fisch, R. (1974). *Change: Principles of Problem Formation and Problem Resolution.* New York: W. W. Norton & Company.

Wells, J. (1985). The group-as-a-whole perspective, and its theoretical roots. In A. D. Colman & M. Giller (Eds.), *Group Relations Reader 2* (pp. 109-126). Washington: A. K. Rice Institution.

Wexler, D. A., & Rice, L. N. (Eds.). (1974). *Innovations in Client-Centered Therapy.* New York: John Wiley & Sons.

Whitaker, C. (1989). *Midnight Musings of a Family Therapist.* New York: W. W. Norton & Company.

Whitaker, C. A., & Bumberry, W. M. (1988). *Dancing with the Family: A Symbolic-Experiential Approach.* New York: Brunner/Mazel.

Whitaker, C. A., & Keith, D. V. (1981). Symbolic-experiential family therapy. In A. S. Gurman & D. P. Kniskern (Eds.), *Handbook of Family Therapy* (pp. 187-225). New York: Brunner/Mazel.

Wienecke, H. (1984). Themenzentrierte Interaktion in einer Ehepaargruppe [Report on a marital therapy group using theme-centered interaction]. *Partnerberatung, 21,* 114-126.

Wolf, A. (1983). Psychoanalysis in groups. In H. I. Kaplan & B. J. Sadock (Eds.), *Comprehensive Group Psychotherapy* (pp. 113-131). Baltimore: Williams & Wilkins.

Wolf, A., & Schwartz, E. U. (1962). *Psychoanalysis in Groups.* New York: Grune & Stratton.

Yalom, I. D. (1975). *The Theory and Practice of Group Psychotherapy.* New York: Basic Books.

NAME INDEX

SUBJECT INDEX